SUBHASH BOSE

India's First Prime Minister?

SUBHASH BOSE

India's First Prime Minister?

Dr U V Singh

PENTAGON PRESS

Subhash Bose: India's First Prime Minister?

Dr UV Singh

ISBN 978-81-8274-930-6

First Published in 2017

Published by
PENTAGON PRESS
206, Peacock Lane, Shahpur Jat
New Delhi-110049
Phones: 011-64706243, 26491568
Telefax: 011-26490600
email: rajan@pentagonpress.in
website: www.pentagonpress.in

Printed at Aegean Offset Printers, Greater Noida, U.P.

This book is dedicated to my grandchildren:
Aditya Vir Singh,
James Leonardo Ripa
and
Anya Ripa

This work is not a biography of India's great revolutionary.

It's an ardent fan's tribute to the great soul.

It's part fact and part fiction.

CONTENTS

ACKNOWLEDGEMENT

My sincerest thanks go to Mr Rajan Arya, the proprietor of Pentagon Press, who persuasively suggested that a book on Subhash Chandra Bose—India's great revolutionary freedom fighter—be done in light of recent developments as well as the historical facts, and also the imaginations and expectations of the people of India.

And my India Habitat Centre colleague, Mr. Iqbal Husain Khan—a learned but low profile intellectual—who undertook the laborious job of reading the manuscript and suggested several alterations, deserves, profuse thanks.

New Delhi, September 2016 **U V Singh**

Jai Hind

PREFACE

To think about Netaji Subhash Chandra Bose today, or for that matter Mahatma Gandhi, is almost like travelling back in a space-time frame, reaching into the mid-1940s when the politico-social atmosphere in India was charged with strange energies of emotions, patriotism and expectations of freedom. Half-clad and barefoot urchins formed the great mass of ***"prabhat pheries"*** (the morning rounds) in the streets of small towns in rural India. A few elders, or senior boys, led the processions with the tricolours of various sizes—-and shouts of ***"Jai Hind", "Bharat Mata Ki Jai", "Netaji Zindabad"*** and "***Mahatma Gandhi amar rahein***" filled the morning air. Hardships like walking through dirty lanes and braving morning chill didn't matter. The energy of patriotism pervaded the whole environment. These were revolutionary activities for the expectant generation. Normally, Sunday was a special occasion for display of the infective patriotism.

Radio was the only source of information in those times. There were only few sets in a village—only *Pradhan* and/or *Numerdar* had the facility of the sound-box. In urban areas, a lot more shopkeepers and Raj officials could afford the magical sound box. A few *paan* and cigarette shops that were often equipped with a radio-set too became centre for listening to the freedom movement news. Newspapers in rural areas were not easy to come by. Postman, whenever he came, was another source of news. And the people who travelled to towns for business or court work were another. The living atmosphere was fully charged; there was no scope for mental and/or social idleness—evening discussions and debates were a full-time activity. In some old rural houses or *havelis*, framed photos or calendar cutouts of national leaders of those times can still be seen hanging on unkempt and dusty walls.

Now in the new century, the situation has changed a great deal. We have been free for over seven decades and information is no more a rarity, thanks to the information revolution that we have experienced in the past 2-3 decades. Yet, names of great revolutionaries or any reading material and visuals on them still churn up great interest in the old generation that had witnessed the turbulent years of the 1940s. Those presently in middle or late seventies can recollect and /or recapture those moments of great thrill and excitement.

And there is another category of young Indians, as well as senior citizens (the author included) who would have loved to have Subhash Chandra Bose as India's first Prime Minister. They feel that, in that event, the situation in the country would have been totally different—possibly a lot better. In their view, we would have become a superpower long back. This book, in view of the author, will serve a great purpose of fuelling interest and emotions of the young dreamers as well as the older ones vis-à-vis India's unique freedom struggle.

New Delhi, September 2016 **U V Singh**

Jai Hind

INTRODUCTION

During the 2014 general elections, India witnessed a strange trend of political one-upmanship. BJP, which was battling to capture power from the incumbency- afflicted UPA, went all out to claim ownership to several major icons of India—the great souls who struggled towards freeing the country from an over-two- centuries-old exploitative British occupation. It couldn't claim Mahatma Gandhi as its own because RSS/Hindutva elements had conspired to kill the ***"Father of the Nation"*** on January 30, 1948. They blamed him for the partition of India and then being sympathetic to Muslims in general, and Pakistan in particular. They always blamed Jawaharlal Nehru for India's disastrous Kashmir policy and the military debacle on the Indo-China border in 1962. All this was acceptable for it was an opposition party that was never able to gain a stable and decisive foothold in the Indian Parliament.

Through the 2014 campaign, they grew desperate to grab political power and the crumbs that would fall in the lap of winners by default. They needed some icons that could help them climb the ladder of power, but they failed to locate any suitable candidate in their own political stables who could energize them and inflate their vote bank to a winning level. The desperation led to a scramble in grabbing national icons of the freedom struggle era with whom the aggressive party and its associates had nothing to do in the past, for over eight-nine decades.

Since the BJP's lead campaigner came with a Gujarati load of experience, they first attempted to own Sardar Vallabbhai Patel—a life-long Congressman and a great Gandhian freedom fighter, and also known as the ***"Iron Man of India"***. In order to cover up the gap of the opposite association, they planned to cast a sky-high statue of the great Sardar with iron pieces collected from villages spread all over India.

Simultaneously, they started to spread the canard that the great Sardar wasn't treated well by Jawaharlal Nehru, or that he wasn't heard on numerous issues of national importance. They forgot to appreciate that the great Sardar was a tough man who didn't need anyone to treat him with kid gloves. He could fight his own battle, and win it too.

The idea was to rekindle the great respect that the Indian masses had for the great Sardar, and turn the same into vote streams. It worked partly in the 2014 general election.

Simultaneously, they had gone for the great dalit leader Dr. B R Ambedakar, who had led the long and arduous exercise of framing India's constitution in the post-independence years. The aggressive band of Hindutva politicians in this case, too, claimed that the "***Father of Indian Constitution***" wasn't treated well by Nehru and his Congress. Their effort to mislead and misinform the public didn't succeed because several political outfits with dalits dominance, especially the BSP and several Ambedkerite groups, were in stiff possession of his legacy. They opposed the Hindutva brigade's efforts with tooth and nail.

During the Bihar assembly election in 2015, while making feeble attempts to win dalits' support employing the name of Ambedakar, they went with full force to claim Jaiprakash Narayan and Babu Rajendra Prasad—both of whom were originally from Bihar. This misadventure too didn't yield them the desired outcome, and the power activists failed miserably. Their tally for the Bihar assembly wasn't respectable enough for a party that ruled at the Center.

A few months later, despite its Bihar debacle, the BJP set its eyes on West Bengal elections that were scheduled for 2016. In this state, BJP didn't have even minimal roots on which to raise its tree of hopes, yet under the shadow of its Delhi rule it wanted to plant itself in light of the opportunity offered by the weakened communists and a disorganized

Congress. The ruling Trinamool Congress (TMC), they thought, suffered from the affliction of incumbency and poor governance. But to be relevant, the BJP needed some local crutches to support its new enterprise here too.

The renowned Bose family of Calcutta has been struggling with the over seven-decades-old myth or controversy of Subhash Bose's death (in a plane crash in August 1945), or his disappearance. Several committees and commissions set up by various governments at the center didn't help a bit. Although the Bose family was deeply divided on the issue, a faction of it always strived for more information on the issue, often blaming the Congress governments for not being helpful—even alleging that Jawaharlal Nehru, the independent India's first Prime Minister, wasn't interested in solving the Bose riddle. Some members even alleged that Nehru government not only kept files on the subject, but went snooping on the iconic family. Lies and hearsay had overtaken the issue.

BJP sensed an opportunity—one: to grow in West Bengal on Bose family's emotional plank, and two: to burrow into the Trinamool Congress' support base in the state. Narendra Modi, the BJP/NDA globe trotter Prime Minister of India, made the first move and met some members of the Bose family in Germany during his official visit to the former fascist state in April 2015.

A few months later, on 15 October, 2015, India's Prime Minister played host to a 30-member strong delegation of the large Bose family at his official residence at 7 Race Course Road, New Delhi. It was a great photo-opp for the PM as well as for the grand-nephews and grand-nieces of the great revolutionary. As expected, he played up the family's demand for declassifying files lying with the Indian government. Acting as an all-powerful PM, he promised to open all the classified files that were gathering dust in the cupboards of the Government of India.

The Indian PM's gesture to the Bose family, when on an official trip to Germany, had alarmed Mamata Banerjee, the Trinamool Congress' chief minister in West Bengal. She felt threatened and sensed danger coming her way. And, in a fast moving reaction, she outwitted the Saffron establishment by declassifying all Bose- related files in September 2015 (the ones that had gathered dust in the 'Writers Building'). All 64 Bose family related files were thrown open to the media, national as well as the state ones.

Some politicians felt that it was the mercurial Mamata's masterstroke in the run-up to the 2016 Bengal elections. These files, which were earlier seen by Justice M K Mukherjee Commission, primarily focused on Subhash Bose's activities in the 1930s and, a second set of them, on the post-independence era pertaining to alleged surveillance of the Bose family.

The Central government had a bigger pile of over 100 files on Bose and related matters, and not to be outdone in the game of vote politics, Narendra Modi's establishment orchestrated a 'files declassification' drama on the 119th birth anniversary of the great nationalist and revolutionary. While the media, TV and press both, went berserk with reporting the event, nothing much came out of the exercise. BJP's main gain was gathering some recall value in minds of mercurial Bengali electorate and a few people, including a senior member of the Bose family, exhibited interest in joining the Saffron bandwagon.

A few months later, when the Election Commission of India announced elections to assemblies of five states, including West Bengal, BJP hurried up to select Chandra Kumar Bose—a great grand nephew of Subhash Bose—as the party's West Bengal face. It wanted to en-cash the residual stock of pro-Bose emotions amongst the mercurial electorate of this state.

The great media blitz thanks to BJP's Central government) that was spawned by the well-timed exercise of files declassification, despite the fact that nothing much (that wasn't already known) came out of it, stressed that there was a need for better understanding Subhash Bose, and putting matters related to the great hero in proper perspective.

And some intellectuals, young and old, tend to dream and speculate as to how situations of governance and development would have unfolded in a free India if Subhash Bose was around and had taken over reins of the government in August 1947 as the first Prime Minister of the newly liberated country. These and numerous related issues propelled the author to come out with the present work.

This small work isn't a biography.

Instead, it's an effort to highlight the persona of India's great hero and understand the challenging circumstances through which he worked, associations that he made, successes that he achieved, mistakes that got committed, his status amongst the great nationalists and revolutionaries of the 20th century, and finally, the cruel fate that robbed him of a great glory by not allowing march of his victorious INA into Delhi.

The last two chapters of this book are fictional in character while the rest represents interpretation and presentation of already reported information on the great revolutionary.

Jai Hind

SECTION I

NON-FICTION

CHAPTER 1

DRAMA OF BOSE'S SECRET FILES

With great fanfare and huge expectations, Narendra Modi government on 23rd January, 2016, and Mamata Banerjee sometime earlier, enacted a great politically designed drama of declassifying secret files on Subhash Chandra Bose. They played to galleries of the Bose family members and his admirers and fans, in addition to the leftist politicians. They had expected great political gains out of this egocentric exercise. Some big skeletons were expected to tumble out of the rotting scraps, tied together with the good old red tape. It was like digging a huge mountain and finding not even a small rat coming out of it. The efforts looked self-serving and truly fruitless.

Attempting to Grab Iconic Legacy

The two egocentric politicians were looking for some massive electoral gains in the next state assembly elections in West Bengal that were scheduled for 2016. They had different or better say, opposing narratives; while Mamata Banerjee wanted to retain her emotions-drenched Bengali voters to again return her motley troublemakers to power, Modi's BJP was trying to find some foothold or roots in this state of mercurial tempers and uncertain outcomes. While Mamata's attempts to claim Bose's legacy looked somewhat acceptable. Modi's gross efforts for garnering or grabbing Bose's legacy looked utterly crude and dishonorable.

Should a good politician fall to such a depth?

In over seven decades of post-independence electoral history of India, BJP never gained any foothold in West Bengal. The political space there, for over the past three decades, was monopolized by communists. Only last time, a mercurial Mamata deprived the aging and increasingly irrelevant communists the bumpy Bengali turf. They weren't able to reinvent themselves; and even today, continue to remain devoid of any fresh energy that could get them again into a fighting mode and be respectable.

And for the BJP, that has been tasting power at the Center with visible inaptitude, partly thanks to Congress' autophagous inaptness, has been looking for ways and means to spread its wings geographically to newer states —West Bengal being one of them. And unfortunately, every time an election falls due, its constituents look for grabbing legacy of one or more great heroes of India, or fall back on debris of Ram temple and Hindutva. For the West Bengal battle of 2016, it wanted to ride the emotional horse of Netaji's legacy.

During the 2014 general elections BJP tried, depending upon location of its campaigns and the demography to grab legacies of B.R. Ambedakar, Sardar Patel, Babu Rajendra Prasad, and even that of Lal Bahadur Shastri in a crude and oppressive manner. To which party these icons belonged, or how their political philosophies didn't gel with that of RSS and/or the BJP, didn't matter a bit. Misinforming people and unprincipled opportunism was their weapon of electoral combats.

In each case, by default, they attempted to say that the Congress had mistreated the subject leaders and didn't give them their due. Subhash Bose was deeply researched, and then reserved as a Brahamastra for the West Bengal elections of 2016.

Little Secret of the Declassified Files

Declassification of secret files that had accumulated with various ministries of the Government of India over the past seven decades on events/queries related to the death or disappearance of Subhash Bose in August 1945 turned out as a great disappointment to the BJP-led NDA government at the Center, and also to the large Bose family. The iconic hero's large family often spoke in differing voices and never looked satisfied with whatsoever the earlier governments had done in this regard. They had great expectations from the said files as well as from the newly-minted benefactors of the Bose family, who had grand designs.

PM Modi's government was looking for 'a large stick in the pile of the old scrap' so that the same could be employed to beat the Congress party red and blue during the upcoming elections in states of Assam and West Bengal. Some elements in the Bose family were looking for some juicy scraps of information, employing which, they could buttress their long-held theory that Nehru attempted to destroy or diminish Subhash Bose's legendry achievements. They, too, were greatly disappointed as nothing of the sort tumbled out of the rotting files. The iconic family's frustrations, over decades, were also magnified by the fact that despite being the prime claimant to the great Bose legacy, they never came near to having a controlling stake in the political environment of the state of West Bengal.

Like hungry wolves, the Indian media (I) devoured contents of the files on 24th January, 2016, i.e. a day after the declassification exercise. All of them vied with each other to report on the matter evening before the multitude of Indian TV channels had gone virtually berserk highlighting opening up of the files.

What came out of the massive effort briefly related to the following?

- Although the declassification advocates viewed it as a very significant event, the long-awaited exercise of opening up the files could not throw any decisive light on Bose's death or disappearance controversy. The controversy stays, and it is bound to continue to kick up dust and grime for many long years to come.
- Since for Mahatma Gandhi, Subhash Bose was a 'prince among patriots', the advocate of non-violence didn't believe the plane crash theory for the legend's death; he didn't even accept Col. Habibur Rahman's testimony in this regard. Gandhi, while talking to waiting journalists, was reported to have said:

"Habib is carrying out his leader's order. I do not believe that Subhash died in any air crash." The great Mahatma was obviously over-taken by the emotional connect that he held for the great revolutionary, despite their methods having differed so widely. Gandhi had the great uncommon capacity to hold people of merit in high esteem even when they differed with him.

- Amiya Nath Bose, Ardhendhu Bose, Surya Kumar Bose and several other members of the large Bose family seemed being interested in further clouding the already opaque myth of Subhash's death or the disappearance story.
- On the other hand, Subhash's daughter Anita Bose Pfaff was clear in her views that her father died on the 18th August, 1945 in a plane crash. Several members of the Bose family, especially Amiya and Ardhendhu, were critical of Anita's views because the same went against their agenda of keeping the myth alive and well-fuelled for many more long years. They had hitched the bandwagon of their social and political interactions to the myth of death or disappearance of the great leader. The mystery served them well; they even negated finding of commissions and committees that were set up by various governments in Delhi to investigate and settle the issue of Bose's death or disappearance. They didn't seem to want any clarity to emerge in this regard.
- Ashes kept in an urn at the Tokyo's RankoJi temple (supposed to be of Subhash Bose) have long been a matter of simmering controversy too. Bose's family has never been interested in getting the great hero's ashes back to the motherland. They didn't want to accept that the most illustrious member of the family had died in an air crash. And the Government of India could not risk the fall-out of bringing home unconfirmed remains of the great hero.
- Anita Bose, Subhash Bose's daughter who settled in Germany, has been of the view that a DNA test should be done on her father's ashes to confirm or discard, once and for all, the relation of the said ashes to the iconic hero. Is it possible to find some strands of DNA in the said ashes? One is not sure before an attempt is made in that direction. Will the Modi government fulfill the wish of the great hero's daughter? It is wholly uncertain because it's not interested in settling the controversy; keeping it green is an advantage to the Saffron establishment. And how the

other members of the great family will react to the suggestion, or the exercise, if and when some concrete efforts are initiated needs to be watched with interest.

- The Indian government often exhibited reluctance to bring the said ashes to India because it would have given no satisfaction to the Bose family—and, for sure, it might have caused some further controversies. So long as the ashes remain in Japan, the government sees room for misgivings and maneuverings that it has not fully accepted findings of various committees and commissions with regard to the great hero's death.
- Whether Bose was viewed as a war criminal by the British authorities or the UN does not get clarified by the opening up of the said files. British government never claimed that the great hero was a war criminal. Only some interested elements have been raising the issue—probably to fuel the myth of the great revolutionary's disappearance.
- A cleverly planted hoax by some anti-Nehru fans of Bose got exposed on account of the files opening exercise too. Some Jawaharlal, not Nehru, reportedly wrote a letter to British Prime Minister saying that "Your war criminal has been allowed to enter Russian territory by Stalin". Its language and spelling mistakes confirmed that someone wanted to play mischief and sully Nehru's spotless reputation. The ease with which RSS and/or Hindutva elements could penetrate the Indian administration, planting of such a mischievous scrap of paper was always possible.
- The files also threw up several misgivings and dark spots about the air crash, of which non-availability of record of the crash, Bose's death, the death certificate of one Okara Ochiro under which the great hero was cremated, ashes kept in a Tokyo temple, demand for DNA test on the hero's remains, drafting of Netaji's death declaration, Shah Nawaz Khan Committee, Khosla Commission and Mukherjee Commission, were important. The theory of air crash seemed turning wholly into a perpetual chaos.
- And the demand for opening up of files that must be resting with foreign governments in Russia, Germany, Britain and Japan, emerged even before the 100 odd files declassified on 23rd January, 2016, were fully read and/or analysed properly.

- Surya Kumar Bose (ii), a grand nephew of Subhash Bose, in his post-files opening interview spewed out the Bose family's accumulated anger or frustration against Congress governments which had consistently maintained that the great revolutionary had died in the 18th August 1945 plane crash. Most of the Bose family members, who were always interested in maintaining that the air crash never occurred but never clarfied where-abouts of Bose if he was alive, were actively hostile to the Congress governments' stand.
- The second round of Bose files declassification by the GOI took place at end of March 2016. It was designed to make some impact on the West Bengal state assembly election in favour of the NDA. A report in The Hindu of April 1, 2016 (ix) had the following printed:

  "Netaji may have survived the air crash"

  Without providing any authenticity, some documents said that his radio broadcasts were heard in December 1945 and January and February 1946. The report further added:

  "These (documents) often being either anecdotes or representations without a name and date—all they may do is to keep alive, by a slender thread, the belief that Netaji survived the crash."

  The said broadcasts were reported to have been picked up by a Bengali official of the then Governor's office in Calcutta, and can't as such be considered authentic.

  Reacting to a query from The Hindu as to whether this file opening adds to our knowledge on Netaji's death—in the context of media reports saying so—Harvard historian and Netaji's biographer and grand nephew Sugata Bose replied to a text message with a single word: ***'none'***.

  The useless exercise enacted by the NDA government with a lot of fanfare was a waste of time for all involved, except the media that got another opportunity to harp on the unsolvable mystery.

And what could be the political fallout of the declassification of Bose files on elections in West Bengal and Assam could not be clear. BJP's efforts to beat Congress with the Bose's files' stick didn't seem to materialize.

Was File Keeping a Mischief?

It was unavoidable for the Government of India to gather and file whatsoever information came its way on India's great hero. The story of Bose being alive—and rumours of he being spotted at all god forsaken places with regular occurrence—were indeed irresistible; the government had to take note of the same. No Prime Minister, as per the author's assessment, needed to ask for information; they regularly fell into the heap through various tentacles of the information agencies, Intelligence Bureau and the rest. And over the period, the same accumulated into a great pile. Hence, files came into being almost by default; the process was unavoidable. And not keeping any files on Bose would have sure been construed being disrespectful to the great icon.

Most of the stories which entered the files were possibly planted and, almost all of them were motivated to garner some attention or demand some favours and/or facilities from the government. The large Bose family, for a variety of reasons, has been fuelling the fires of the great hero's death and disappearance-related myth. Some of them wanted political mileage, positions on various committees and commissions formed for answering the misgivings regarding the great hero, and much more. Some others wanted to win elections, and there were also those who desired statues of Bose to be erected at place of their choice. Naming roads, lanes and institutions after the great hero—and declaration of holidays etc., was an attention-grabbing game for several of the family's politically-excited members. Bengali politicians and fans, not related to the family, were not far behind in keeping alive the myth of Bose's death/ disappearance either. Several members of the Indian Parliament made regular contributions in this regard.

Bose, as is well-known, was part of a crowded household of 11 siblings[1] in a rich Bengali family of Cuttack (some sources have reported the number of siblings to be 13). They all grew up struggling for space and attention, and branched into different professions, marrying and producing an impressive crop of nephews and nieces. The family, on account of Bose having married an Austrian lady, had extended beyond the physical geography of India. And with regards to Subhash Bose, the great political icon, almost each of them had a separate objectivity and/or agenda. Their choices were:

- To accept the 18th August 1945 plane crash theory
- To debunk the plane crash
- To promote disappearance myth
- And then support the great icon's being sighted at odd places in Russia, Central Asia and even in the Gangetic plains of India

They debated the matter in great details and ***'Forward Bloc'*** elements and associated fringe elements doggedly pursued and fuelled the fallacies.

So, when his daughter Anita Pfaff accepted that her father had indeed died in a plane crash, others of the family differed. Her assertion seemed to topple the apple cart of some Bose family members. They wanted to continue milking the ***'Bose Mystery's Holy Cow'***. Some felt that he couldn't die—and others hypothesized that he lived somewhere as a watchful *sanyasi*. The attention that they got every time the great hero's name cropped up in any story in print or any other media mesmerized them. It was too difficult for them to accept the truth, since the myth of his disappearance had assumed '***addictive proportions***'.

Why files were kept and why the same weren't made public wasn't understandable; its logic didn't appeal them. They saw conspiracies in everything that happened or was assumed to have happened.

As recently as the middle of February 2016, some members of the Bose family travelled to Lucknow to meet Chief Minister Akhilesh Yadava (iv), and requested him to investigate reports that one **"Gumnami Baba"** roamed the plains of Uttar Pradesh— who some people claimed was nobody else but Subhash Bose in disguise. It seemed to cross limits of absurdity of blind faith in the myth of disappearance of the great hero. News highlight and publicity seems the objective irrespective of....

Committees and commissions headed by imminent personalities didn't satisfy numerous members of the Bose family. Some loopholes or disagreements could always be raised. Acceptance of truth would have amounted to loss of the myth, and that wasn't acceptable to the interested elements within the family, or those outside it.

Suresh Bose, an elder brother of Subhash, was part of the Shah Nawaz Khan Committee, who travelled widely and spent months looking for truth regarding the August 18, 1945 air crash. Several eyewitness accounts, even that of Col. Habibur Rahman who had travelled with Bose in the ill-fated plane and was one of the last persons to have seen the great hero alive, weren't relied upon. His cherished aim wasn't to bury the controversy. He had to keep the mystery of crash and/or disappearance green and alive, in fitness of things that suited the family's calculations.

The 100-odd files which had accumulated a lot of trash over seven decades while lying in custody of the Central government were declassified (put in public domain) by the BJP government on 23rd January 2016—the 119th birth anniversary of the great hero—with a lot of fanfare. There were huge expectations but nothing much that wasn't already known came out of the exercise.

Ignoring the files declassification exercise (long demanded by the Bose family), a nephew of Bose named Ardhendu Bose rubbished the plane crash theory, calling it a cover-up by Japan with the purpose of letting the war hero escape.

As per a report (iv) in the Indian Express dated 25th January 2016, Ardhendu was reported to have said:

> *"There was no plane crash. The British government created propaganda (of the crash). It (the crash theory) was a cover-up created by Japan to help Netaji."*

How the two adversary governments—the Japanese and British—collaborated in the said cover-up, wasn't clarified by Ardhendu. His agenda vis-à-vis the files seemed not only to keep the controversy well-fuelled but to expand and complicate the mystery.

Netaji Files: No End to the Mystery

Netaji Subhash Chandra Bose's 119th birth anniversary that fell on 23rd January 2016 was significant for the reason that Narendra Modi's NDA government, as it was threatening for long, declassified a 100 odd secret files kept on Bose-related matters by various governments in the past seven decades.

A few months earlier, Modi had hosted a 30 members' delegation from the large Bose family at his official 7 Race Course Road residence in New Delhi. Expectations were raised sky-high as if some huge mystery was to be laid open to the public; and that the blame for misdeeds, if any, could straightway be placed at Congress's door. The whole event of files' declassification turned into a non-event. It was expected that the files would confirm that Netaji didn't die in a plane crash on 18 August, 1945; and that he lived incognito somewhere in Russia or Central Asia, or even as a *sanyasi* in India; that the Nehru government of 1950s and 60s had conspired to cause such a situation.

The files revealed nothing to serve these wild expectations and/or insinuations; even the expectant Indian press looked disappointed. An editorial commentary (in this regard) in the The Asian Age in its 25th January issue (v), amongst others, commented:

> *"....but it's an irony that despite the files now being public, no clear evidence has emerged on whether the iconic hero who waged war to free his country survived or died in the 1945 air crash near Taipei. Only one 1945 Cabinet note states his death took place, but without any new evidence."*
>
> *"In many ways, the enduring Bose mystery will perhaps never be solved. Numerous commissions haven't been able to fit all pieces of the puzzle together, nor has the government's action of placing the declassified files in the public domain made anyone wiser."*
>
> *"The Bose mystery will thus live on: people will remain free to believe the nationalist hero is still, defying all laws of Nature, alive somewhere!"*

In view of the author, the Bose mystery, very much like the Indo-Pak conflict, has assumed intractable permanence. It can't be solved as there are interested elements whose existence necessitates that the controversy be kept alive for their survival and well-being. Like the lovers of the two nation theory in Pakistan continue to propagate that India poses an existential threat to their country, some Bose family members and fans seem fully convinced that the Nehru-Gandhi combine was hell-bent upon obliterating the great hero's memory and contributions. Both the situations are based on untenable falsehood.

And any attempt to decode the great Subhash Bose mystery is destined to turn like watering a Neem tree—since whatsoever care one takes of it, in final analysis, it ends up giving only some small bitter fruits. Nothing big or sweet shall ever come out of it.

Attempt to Blame Nehru

Several members of the huge Bose family, over the period of decades, seemed fascinated with blaming Nehru for Bose's disappearance mystery. Ardhendu Bose (iv), a Mumbai-based businessman from a distinguished textile family, in his interview to the Indian Express (as reported in its 25th January 2016 issue) was specifically reported to have said that the family believed Jawaharlal Nehru wanted to ***"wipe out the memory of Subhash Chandra Bose and INA"*** due to their rivalry.

It was indeed a misconstrued statement designed to garner public sympathy while available proof was clear about the fact that Bose and Nehru, both belonged to the same leftist faction of the Congress. Bose's disappearance act (if he really didn't die in the air crash) must have been of his own choice. Nehru could not have created it. Criticism of Nehru by some Bose family members and sundry politicians in West Bengal has been a desperate act to gather attention.

Nehru stayed loyal to his socialistic developmental philosophy through whole of his life while Bose had hobnobbed with a variety of communists and fascists.

Historians, Indian as well as foreign, reject Ardhendu's contention and are clearly of the opinion that there are no reasons for implicating Nehru in fabricating the plane crash episode (if there was any). B K Prasad, professor of History at Bilaspur Central University who claimed to have for long researched the Bose myth, was reported to have said:

> *"There is no existing record of the crash. I do not hold the opinion that there was no crash, but mere absence of record does not prove there was no crash."*

Prasad went further and elaborated:

> *"Why would Japan decide to create this cover-up? Is there any record?*

Why would Netaji seek asylum in USSR? He had already allied with the axis powers. Do you think Netaji would suddenly disappear, never contact his family or any known person after 18 August, 1945? Aren't we denigrating leader of his caliber by saying that he suddenly began living like a masked fugitive?

The irony is, once you believe there was no plane crash, you can have any number of conjectures without any evidence."

Ardhendu wasn't the only Bose family member to have deliberately spiked the controversy of the great leader's death/disappearance. Several of his nephews and nieces fell to the trap of contradicting the plane crash incident just to garner limelight, or to bring to fruition some hidden agenda. Politics in the large Bose family was intense and Bengali politicians in general, and Trinamool and BJP ones in particular, encouraged such tendencies at times of elections.

No Evidence of Snooping

The declassified files threw up no evidence of snooping on the Bose family by any government. The British system of information gathering could not have changed or disappeared the very next day in 1947. It seems, the charge of snooping, often fabricated by biased politicians, received no ground out of the subject files. It is easy to assign mythical formations and contrive that Nehru feared Bose's return to India in the post-independence period.

There is no evidence popping out of the said files that Nehru demanded or ordered any snooping; it is just a fabricated formation of interested elements.

Bose wasn't a child, nor was he a simpleton; he wasn't ever scared of conflict or ran from a fight. So to presume that he didn't return to India in order to avoid conflict, or that Nehru so desired, is a well-fabricated fallacy and insult to the great leader's capabilities.

CHAPTER 2

POLITICAL PHILOSOPHY OF BOSE

Outside the non-violent sphere of Mahatma Gandhi, Subhash Chandra Bose has been the most admired revolutionary of modern India. He is loved and admired by all Indians—urban or rural, literate or illiterate, Bengalis or non-Bengalis. The 1940s and 1950s generations of Indians were deeply in love with him. In those days, a majority of students in hostels and dormitories kept his framed photo on the wall of their rooms. And he was the most popular calendar feature of those times.

His name and the slogan of *'Azad Hind'* was enough for perpetual deluge of emotions. His fans weren't limited to a class, caste or religion; he was a universal hero for Indians. Even those who disagreed with him, or on his methodology, had tremendous respect for him. Some have raised him to the stature of a deity without even studying his life and/or works in any meaningful details. On account of his militant nationalism, Indians' love for him continued to go viral and, despite over seven decades of his escape from British captivity, it hasn't diminished a bit.

Subhash Bose is a Timeless Hero

Although Bose was a Congressman for over 16 years and after running into an open conflict with Mahatma Gandhi, he founded *'Forward Bloc'*, initially as a pressure group within the Congress. Currently, newly invigorated political outfits like BJP and Trinamool Congress are striving hard to claim his legacy, just to exploit Indian masses' ever-green adoration and adulations for the great revolutionary. In view of this, for intellectuals and the erudite, it becomes necessary to explore and understand his political thoughts and/or philosophy with deeper precision.

Political philosophy of Bose didn't gel well with the non-violent, non-cooperation and *Swadeshi* struggle of Mahatma Gandhi and the Indian National Congress (INC) that, as a massive decades' long movement, was collectively called *Satyagraha*. Bose was a restless patriot; he wanted quick departure of British imperialists from India.

He wasn't much of a democrat to suit the working philosophy of Congress. His urge for speed of action and quick results coloured him as an autocratic and authoritarian leader. This nature of him had come to light right during his early association with the national party that, under Gandhi and Nehru's guidance, was spearheading the campaign for India's independence.

Initial Influences on Bose

Like most of the post-WW I intellectuals, Bose too initially put his faith in socialism; and with time, drifted to fascism via the unstable route of communism. Throughout his eventful political career, he found inspiration in European revolutionary history and associated activism. He was particularly influenced by the Italian revolutionary named Giuseppe Garibaldi. Locally, Lok Manya Tilak and CR Das had caught his admiration. Tilak was the first Indian leader to directly call for and encourage use of violence against occupiers of India. He had a great following, and the British were deeply scared of him. Subhash Bose became Tilak's fan at an early age.

CR Das was a renowned Bengali lawyer and along with Motilal Nehru, founded the Swaraj Party in 1923; since after the Gaya conference in 1922, Congressmen were divided on the non-cooperation movement that deeply engaged freedom fighters of all hues. They were divided into ***"Changers"*** and ***"Non-changers"*** i.e. those wanting to give-up the non-cooperation and end boycott of legislatures. The other group wanted to continue with the non-cooperation as part of the independence struggle.

CR Das headed the Changers group, who wanted to stop boycott, fight elections and enter legislatures for introducing changes from within.

On Gandhi's advice, Bose came under Das' mentorship.

Subhash Bose's education in history and political thought had skilled him in the art and science of revolution. That is why, despite deep admiration, he was uncomfortable in the company of Gandhi and Nehru all through his almost over one-and-a half decade long association with them. He wanted to apply the tool of violent revolution and consequent social upheaval for freeing India from the tight clutches of the British imperialism. He wanted an active conflict with the force of which the British could be pushed out of India.

But his covert and overt strivings in this direction got frustrated by the massive force of passivity of the Gandhian *Satyagraha*. His persistent orientation towards employment of militant tools cautioned Congress on one hand, and scared the Raj administrators on the other. He made frequent rounds of the British jails.

Bose's half-hearted efforts to organize his followers into a grouping known as ***'Forward Bloc'*** did not yield desired results. For whatever reasons, he couldn't or didn't organize them on militant lines. Here, he didn't follow Garibaldi who, with a small band of just 60 revolutionaries in his mobile outfit, had fought opposing forces and succeeded in finally rejuvenating Italy into a united nation. Bose and his ***'Forward Bloc'*** followers couldn't stir the Indian masses to a fervency needed for igniting a militant revolution. And in the author's assessment, adequate inputs in terms of training and equipment weren't infused either.

Deficiency of Planning and Organization

In addition to the inputs needed for a militant approach to succeed in a large country that had suffered under a strong colonial grip, effective planning was missing too.

The requisite elements of ***'planning, organizing, leading and control'*** for effectively initiating, intensifying and retaining a massive militancy were not assembled well enough.

Bose wasn't a trained military man, and hence, he couldn't put together an effective organization (or a fighting machine) of committed followers to ensure that the task of militant revolution took route of success. Unlike Fidel Castro and Mao Zedong, he never consolidated his military thoughts and strategies into locally productive actions. Short-term as well as long-term plans (STPs and LTPs) were never put together. He probably didn't fathom the enormity of planning and resources needed for militarily pushing the Raj forces out of India.

Bose's working philosophy primarily centered or rested upon the quadrangle of *'socialism, swadeshi, secularism and swaraj'*, which he wanted to implement through the route of an authoritarian administration. An armed struggle to push the British out of India was often on his mental screen, but he couldn't give it a practical form. There were several reasons for the same. Most importantly, he hoped that anti-British forces of Europe could be enticed to help him to do the job. However, it was the '*crucial strategic deficiency*' of his plans for pushing the Raj out of India. His plans were mostly plutonic as they lacked reality-based planning. He hadn't, for sure, done a SWOT analysis for himself in relation to the massive adversary that he faced. For him, emotions possibly over-ruled the hard facts of life.

He was also convinced that an *'authoritarian centralized governance'* or socialism would save Indian masses from post- revolutionary unrest; unlike the one that had occurred in France in the last two decades of the 19th century—the post-revolution period.

He dreamt into too distant a future... while the first need for '*ways and means*' analysis and planning that was needed to fuel the revolution that he strived for—and push the British occupiers out of the motherland—weren't adequately attended to, or planned for.

Environment of Bose's Early Life

Bose had grown up in the post-1905 'agitation intense environment' that had gripped the Bengali society on account of partition of the state of Bengal and Raj's refusal to undo the mischief. Agitation against partition of Bengal was spearheaded primarily by the Hindu upper class and intellectuals of the region. They petitioned to Lord Curzon, the then Viceroy of India, but were disappointed by his refusal to undo the decision. *Hartals* and agitations turned frequent in occurrence—and, as a consequence, while businesses didn't open, several agitationists resorted to hunger strikes. While Raj administration ignored the rising storm, the leadership, primarily constituting of Hindus businessmen and intellectuals, called for *'swadeshi'* that included active boycotting of British goods.

Soon, it became a movement and subsequently, Congress' push gave it a cutting-edge advantage. Calcutta businessmen, along with many others all over the country, cancelled their import orders for British textiles. Once the movement gained pace, Muslims and other communities extended their full support. Stocks ready for shipment at Manchester and allied locations were blocked, giving a terrible shock to the British textile trade. Curzon, too, was stunned by the sharp impact—the Indians' new-found capacity to hurt the British left the Raj deeply worried.

Although initially the boycott wasn't planned for long-term action, its efficacy turned it otherwise. While British textile merchants appealed to 10 Downing Street, Bengali activists made huge bonfires of their imported clothing and other goods. The protest became pan-Indian, extending to other imported items of daily use. Even locals commenced making their own salt, despite restrictions on such an indulgence.

In the first two decades of the 20th century, under the garb of revolutionary activities, Swadeshi activists planted seeds of violence, crime and social evils like looting and dacoities. Its influence over Indian society travelled far and wide—even a distant Punjab couldn't escape from its isolated sprinklings.

As an adolescent student, Subhash Chandra Bose couldn't escape absorbing some of its implications. As a result of the charged environment, seeds of patriotism and revolution had taken effective roots in several young minds, and the sensitive soul of Bose absorbed a lot of it.

In the meantime, Ideas of Russian revolution, too, had filtered into the restless Indian society; the impact was especially deep in Bengal; and Bose, too, couldn't escape being influenced by the same. Initially, he wavered between socialism and communism. He didn't have Lenin's and Stalin's dogmatism to initiate and mature a political philosophy based upon his leftist leanings.

During second and third decades, under Gandhi's non-violent movement, Swadeshi became the most potent tool in India's struggle for Independence. Since it directly tormented the British, Subhash (during his initial political exposure) became substantially enthusiastic about the Gandhian movement.

Gandhi's 'charkha and spinning and weaving' of indigenous clothing became a sort of a religion for all Congressmen and freedom fighters, several of whom vowed to wear only self-spun and self-woven cloth called ***'Khadi'***.

Nehrus of Allahabad, an aristocratic family of substantial means, turned to Khadi; all leading members of the Indian National Congress followed the trend. Khadi, thus, overtook India's independence movement and the post-independence political brigade fell into its tight grip for a long time. The sartorial grip of khadi continued well into the second decade of the new century, and with Modi's uncommon blessing, it shows no signs of weakening.

Expression of Socialism and Secularism

Bose's secularism during his INA years (1943 to 1945) was brightly evident in composition of this unique fighting force and its leadership. A large number of Muslims, Buddhists and Sikhs settled in East Asia; and those amongst the soldiers of British Indian Army, who fell into hands of Japanese, had joined the legendry INA.

Was his secularism endemic to his personality or during his INA years it became a default product of circumstances?

He had to pick up his combatants out of the available East Asian populace that had been exploited a great deal by the European imperialists on one hand, and the surrendered soldiers of the British Indian Army on the other. Both the groups had active anti-British and anti-imperialistic sentiments. Hence, based upon the short history of INA and its composition, it wouldn't be safe to conclude that our great hero was a '***well-baked socialist or secularist***'. He had experienced and/or worked through communist and fascist forces of that time. He admired Lenin and Stalin for having turned a backward peasant group of states into an industrialized superpower.

Subhash didn't have the patience of Gandhi and Nehru, nor did he fully trust the efficacy of non-violent struggle. He wasn't a philosopher, and in the socio-political environment that he grew up, there was little chance for him to appreciate and absorb silent vitalities of non-violence.

Furthermore, the brutal force of British administration was a great hindrance for Bose in furthering of his revolutionary agenda, which he hadn't probably anticipated with adequate measure. Frustrated with frequent arrests and imprisonments in early 1941, he smuggled himself out into the embrace of European fascism.

In fact, well in advance of his dramatic escape from India, Bose's focus seemed to have shifted from revolution in general to fascism in particular. He was impressed by how Germany and Italy had challenged allied powers, collectively represented by Britain, France, USA and their other associates.

Volume of Western literature suggested that Bose believed in feasibility of worldwide Zeitgeist—including that of India. It called for spread and/or adoption of fascism on a wide scale. His enthusiasm for Nazi-militarism was obvious, which probably led Western historians and commentators to showcase Bose's love for fascism. On the other hand, many writers, particularly the ones from the subcontinent, believed that Bose, till the very last, looked forward to India's post-colonial development through application of tools and methodologies of socialism.

Ways and Means Clarity

Ways and means clarity, irrespective of his direction and choice was Bose's perpetual strength. *Swaraj* or freedom was most important for him, and means to achieve the same were to depend upon situations and challenges encountered.

Unlike Mahatma Gandhi, he had no ways and means confusion or sanctity. For him, any means or any mix of the same that could push the British out of India was good enough. In this respect, he was nearer to the legendry Chanakya than the moralist Mahatma. But he didn't seem to possess the skills and patience of the great guru of Moriyan kings, or even that of the illustrious Mahatma.

Preference for ***'authoritarian militancy'***, advocacy of collective socialism and finally merging with the fascism of axis powers didn't bother him; if they did, he found ways to justify the same to his inner-self on one hand, and to his colleagues and followers on the other. In a way, through this choice, he showed massive strength of character and capacity to deal with difficult situations as a master tactician too. As far as his objective and its attainments were concerned, he was more akin to warrior Karna, the great mythological character from the Mahabharata era. Karna never deviated from his aim of defeating Arjuna—his proclaimed adversary—but the fate had willed otherwise. Bose and Karna, both had associated with powers that were destined to be defeated. Both were tragic heroes of their individual situations.

As stated earlier, Bose, during his over one-and-a-half decade long association with the INC, never looked comfortable with the Gandhian thoughts and methodology—broadly called Satyagraha. Unable to persuade Mahatma towards his radical line of action and also not succeeding to sway majority of Congressmen in direction of his own militant philosophy, he resigned from the presidency of INC in April 1939. A month later, he founded ***'Forward Bloc'***—a faction within the Congress itself.

Forward Bloc was a product of frustration of Bose and his leftist associates, and hence, it never gained decisive grounds. After Bose escaped to Europe, the freshly-minted organization suffered a loss of leadership. No one amongst its members had charisma and/or foresight to fill the gap that occurred on account of Subhash's departure.

The British took a serious note of founding of Bose's militant organization and outpourings of its members at its Nagpur conference, just a year after its birth. The British were already under great stress with the commencement of the WW II skirmishes in Europe, and hence, they didn't see emergence of a militant outfit in India—which was a great source of recruits as well as supplies for fighting a great war, as a good omen. They arrested Bose, initially putting him in the Presidency jail and then shifting him to house arrest.

While in detention, Bose must have deliberated in depth, and most probably, didn't find adequate confidence in his newly-minted outfit's capability to wage a successful militant campaign that could turn compelling enough for the British to run out of India. He gave up on utility of the ***'Forward Bloc'*** from the stand-point of his primary objectivity. Bose, quite possibly, came to realize that his ***'Forward Bloc'*** activists were no good for an armed struggle against the disciplined and capable British imperialists; and that, for the purpose, he needed outside help.

Whether founding of the '***Forward Bloc***' was a knee-jerk decision or adequate planning had gone into it, never became clear. Leave apart running a revolution, it never even got to becoming a durable political force. It never captured power even in its home state of West Bengal.

Had Bose not founded the '***Forward Bloc***' and stayed in the Congress, expressing his deviant views but being cooperative with Gandhi, there would have been no need for him to fall in the fascist black hole. In that situation, as the most charismatic leader of the independence struggle era, he sure would have been Gandhi's choice to lead the independent India as its first PM.

And with his matchless dialogue and diplomatic skills, he could have possibly prevailed upon MA Jinnah not to insist upon the destructive form of the ***"two nations theory"***.

In early 1941, he escaped from house detention and proceeded to Soviet Union via Afghanistan. Here, too, he found Stalin cold to the idea of investing military resources to help liberate India. The great dictator saw no tangible benefit or low hanging fruits in assisting Bose and committing to his proposal of uncertain outcome. Possibly, Bose's plans weren't impressive enough—or the seasoned dictator saw no benefit in antagonizing the British who, at that time, were the greatest empire in the world.

Bose's Over-optimism

Bose seemed to have suffered from over-optimism about the Nazi-Germany's military capabilities too; he misjudged and over-estimated the Germans' capacity and intentions. His critical assessment was blurred on account of (a) that it was an ardent enemy of Britain that had occupied India for almost two centuries, and (b) that an enemy's enemy looked an obvious friend, or a likely source of assistance.

Was Hitler India's friend (in need) in any true sense, or did he see Bose as just an anti-British publicity point? The Goebbelist mindset of Germans was indeed aggressively infective.

Germany or any other country, howsoever powerful, could not have succeeded against rest of the world, or the allied powers of that time. Secondly, Germans could never be benevolent enough to fight the British just for liberating India; its territorial aim did not fit the situation related to South-Asia. Germany's '**karamchetra or kurukchetra**' was primarily limited to Europe—or it could even extend to part of Africa. To hope that Germany would commit its hard-pressed forces and resources for liberating India and then hand over the territory to Bose, or his tribe, was just a pipe-dream which Bose, erroneously, happened to entertain.

Even before and during the first WW, Indians had pursued Germany for help towards freeing India from the imperialistic grip of Britain. But the response was never bold enough to make a material difference. Kaiser Wilhelm II had even sponsored a cell of Indian radicals who meekly plotted to overthrow the British government or the Raj, as it was then called.

The fact was that the Kaiser was never comfortable with the idea of colonial natives fighting for independence, and he never fully understood and appreciated those seeking the German assistance.

The Germans had several colonies of their own and didn't want to speed up the process of colonial subjects revolting successfully. But wartime demands had forced German administration to have some dealings with radical Indians who persisted with demand for help. Various agencies assisted them—even coordination amongst Indian students and activists was attempted. In some cases, even sending some material assistance to radical elements in India, was resorted to.

They even played with the idea of forming surrendered Indian soldiers into some organized force. But scale of the effort was too feeble and inconsequential, and the Indian radicals weren't organized enough, or lacked capabilities to make good use of the same. As a result, the situation didn't help Germans develop necessary confidence for any more active involvement. And with their defeat in the WW I, German interest in India evaporated quickly.

Hence, despite the fact that Bose was more impressive and persistent in his advocacy for help, Germans were doubly cautious and didn't come anywhere near to the Indian revolutionary's expectations. Germans' virulent racism and absence of Hitler's direct interest in India frustrated Bose. But having had no other options, he persisted with his pestering and insistence.

By middle of the Great War, Germans' incapability to succeed against the allied forces became visible, and it made Bose see light of the situation that was to finally emerge a lot more clearly.

In early period of the war, Bose had predicted German victory but the great revolutionary was either biased or didn't factor in how American entry into the war in support of the British was to change the whole scenario. Several great leaders in the history made errors of judgment, and Bose wasn't an exception.

His long-held perception had possibly clouded his judgment. His predictions almost invariably turned out to being wrong.

In general, all through 1941 and 42, Bose seemed to have suffered a 'cold reception in Germany'. After his escape from Calcutta house arrest in 1941, he hadn't reached Germany directly. He travelled through Soviet Union where Stalin, a shroud politician, cold-shouldered him. Bose was given a transit visa for a short period. The great dictator didn't see merit in Bose's pleadings for military help. He saw no strategic benefits in buying a fight with the mighty British Empire. Even otherwise, for any forays into India, his forces would have needed to first fight the British in Afghanistan and then clearing the same out of India didn't seem an easy task. The Soviets needed to be prepared to face the Nazis and Japanese on their Western and Eastern frontiers respectively. And Stalin's administration had no evidence that Bose's followers in India could organize themselves strongly enough to dislodge the British; even if some material and/or technical assistance was provided to the Indian revolutionaries.

A disappointed Bose had dragged himself half-heartedly to an uncertain reception in Nazi Germany. He was aware of his earlier disappointments with the fascist nation. From 1933 to 1938, during his various forays into Europe, Bose had tried his best to contact Nazi officials at various levels but encountered no good luck for enticing them to come to his rescue. Observing neutrality, or unconcern towards British colonial matters, the Germans had politely rejected his proposals.

In 1941, after the Soviet rebuff, he had no choice but to knock at the Nazis' doors again. And by this time, the Germans were already deep in the WW II engagements. Additionally, Bose was now a lot better prepared in presenting the strategic value of India for the axis powers too.

He had also burnt his boat as far as return to India was concerned; he couldn't come home without risking immediate arrest and imprisonment. He had to make good of the bad situation that he had landed himself into.

Soon Hitler's hatred for the British and his desire to destroy them had intensified too, forcing him to set aside his esteem for the Empire. The Nazi apparatus now saw great propaganda value in Bose and his anti-British fulminations. And despite the fact that the Nazis never committed to the cause of freeing India, they established Bose into the ***'Free India Center'***.

Finding some anchorage, Bose was greatly enthused and he made impressive broadcasts to Indians, or whosoever bothered to listen, suggesting that the axis powers would help liberate India. Noting Bose's enthusiasm, Berlin expanded his role in August 1942 by designating him as '***Commander of the Indian Legion***'—a ragtag assemblage of British Indian soldiers who had surrendered during Germans' North African campaigns.

Bose had difficulty assessing worth of such an assembly of defeated and demoralized soldiers—and soon, numerous mutinies and resultant confusion over the Legion's utility damaged the great Indian revolutionary's reputation with the Nazis, who themselves by now were coming under great stress on account of the resilience of allied powers.

While Bose's own credibility turned doubtful, Nazis suffered several setbacks in the Great War, which compelled them to reconsider their interest in the inconvenient Indian guest. They had committed the blunder of attacking Russia. Possibly, the Nazis also suspected that Bose was a Russian agent.

The first INA attempt had thus failed to bear any desired fruits. Another avatar of INA was almost simultaneously attempted in the East Asia under leadership of one Mohan Singh and Ras Behari Bose. On account of multilateral bunglings, this attempt had failed too. And only in the third form, the INA succeeded under Bose's dynamic leadership.

Worsening of relations with the Nazis didn't enlighten Bose to the futility of jumping from one fascist boat to another. All through 1942, Bose was conveying to his Nazi contacts his desire to move out to the East and work there with the Japanese who, at that stage of the war, seemed more successful against the British in East Asia.

Here, Bose made two mistakes in assessing the prevailing international political scenario: he mistook fascists' crusade for anti-imperialism and also, in presuming that while European fascist forces were faltering, the Nipponese fascists would win against the allied powers… and that the latter would deliver a British-free India to him.

That the Japanese were equal or even more ruthless imperialists than the British didn't occur to him, or he preferred to hope for the best. In fact, Tokyo had merely planned to replace the European colonial powers in the Orient, which they saw as their area of exclusive dominance. The atrocities committed by them in Korea and China had by now become well-known. Bose ignored the situation, or had no option but to ignore it.

Japanese had implemented a carefully crafted deception by choosing local leaders to do their bidding in territories that they had grabbed. They needed an impressive Indian face for effective propaganda against the British. By end of December 1942, they had lost value of Indian face known as Mohan Singh—an obscure Army man who was initially used by them as an Indian face, but had now become inconvenient to continue with.

Bose fitted the bill exceptionally well, and they encouraged him to move East.

Bose's Struggle in the Orient

Bose was enthused by prospects of working with the Japanese; they were winning all over the East and South-East Asia and could, any moment, foray into India.

Bose loved winning situations and, much like a fly that carelessly moves into a spider's nest, he fell into Tokyo's embrace. Nazis arranged for his secret boat journey to the East, midway transferring him to a Japanese vessel. Despite the arduous journey, Bose was enthusiastic for the new mission.

In spurt of enthusiasm, Bose now addressed as Netaji, vigorously condemned the British in his speeches, radio talks and editorials. To exhilaration of Tokyo, Hindus, Muslims, Buddhists, Sikhs and all other Indian communities in East-Asia seemed to lose their traditional differences—uniting under the newly-minted leadership of their Netaji. They proclaimed themselves as a united Indian community.

By now, Indian prisoners of war and volunteers of Indian origin were already being organized into an Indian National Army (the 3rd edition of INA), and Bose enthusiastically took-over its command. By March 1944, under Bose's enthusiastic guidance, the INA marched across South-

East Asia and crossed into India from Burma. It had some initial successes but soon with diminishing Japanese fortunes, was defeated by the determined and better-equipped allies at Kohima and Imphal.

Bose didn't surrender with his INA fighters, which was possibly the biggest mistake of his eventful revolutionary career.

All the captured/surrendered INA fighters—about 12,000 in number—were shifted to various camps in India. Their leaders and commanders faced intense prosecutions at Red Fort in Delhi, wherein Nehru and a galaxy of other prominent Indian lawyers pleaded their case. Prominent INA leaders and commanders were convicted with imprisonment and deportation—but punishment, in whatsoever cases awarded, wasn't implemented for fear of public reaction, mutinies and revolts in armed forces.

Had Bose been with the captive INA soldiers and officers, he sure wouldn't have been hung, or put under long imprisonment.

British were now in a hurry to depart from India. The Great War had weakened them a lot, and they no longer had faith in the loyalty of Indian forces that had protected the Raj all through its long innings in India. Right in 1946, British establishment had decided to vacate India after bifurcating it through creation of Pakistan.

But unfortunately, by now, India had lost its great revolutionary due to post war exigencies.

Ammunition of Emotions

Bose was a supremely gifted leader with a magical capability to play up emotions; to use emotions as ammunition. His radio talks from Berlin and Singapore (1941 to 45) were blasts of pure emotions. Bose had prepared a top secret document titled Berlin in April 1941.

About it, Marshal Getz[1] said:

> *"....proposed an official alliance between India and Axis. In it he described the clandestine operations to occur in Europe and Asia, much of it to be accomplished with Indian sweat and skills, but with Axis*

support. He bolstered the credibility of his offer with the historical and contemporary political evidence, while firing the emotions through the brash use of strongly worded opinion. He analyzed the karma of the Raj, while predicting the future of "Mother Hind". He summed up world politics and showed the Germans how to move into niche Britain seemed destined to leave. The German Foreign Office listened carefully to what Bose had to say."

Three things flow out of the above:

1. Germans did listen carefully but what they thought of it and acted upon wasn't enough for Bose's dreams to come true.
2. Bose sure wasn't good at predicting the future.
3. Bose's followers back home didn't organize themselves well to turn his words into solid deeds.

Impulsive Predictions

Bose had a tendency to talk far deep into the future without supportive logic of ground work. British didn't vacate any niche and the Axis powers suffered a terrible defeat. For a good statesman, a lot of ground work and organizing—and not opening his cards before time—is of paramount importance. Bose suffered from credibility gap, and this kind of forecasting didn't help the said gap to narrow effectively.

Bose believed in "***Axis – Hind Brotherhood***", which didn't really happen in any meaningful way.

At the home front, too, Bose had fallen to needless forecasting.

He spoke more about democracy than socialism during the initial period of his Congress presidency. But soon, during his 2nd term, he moved to far left. He demanded India's freedom in six months and for the purpose, issued an ultimatum, which along with him getting closer to the European fascism caused further rift in the Congress.

He clashed with Gandhi and predicted: ***"If we come to parting of the ways, a bitter civil war will commence."***

He had probably over-read in the leftists' strength since most of them, at that moment of history, were under the spell of Russian communism and its initial successes.

More often than not, he proved that the temperamental revolutionary wasn't good at making predictions; most emotion-driven people aren't good at such activities.

Jai Hind

CHAPTER 3

UNDERSTANDING BOSE'S STRUGGLE

Most Indians—his fans, followers and otherwise—only have a rudimentary understanding of the great revolutionary's struggle. They have only an emotional connect. Here, we attempt to go a little deep into the matter.

Assessment of INA's Imphal Campaign

INA was the first Indian fighting force that entered East India, defeating British Indian Army. As evident from Bose's own assessment, he looked satisfied with the performance of his forces; he was reported to have observed:

> *"The first phase of our campaign is over. Our victorious troops, fighting side by side with Nipponese troops, have pushed back the enemy and are now fighting bravely on the sacred soil of our dear motherland."*

Netaji had further added:

> *"We should have but one desire today so that India may live—the desire to face a martyr's death so that the path to freedom may be paved with martyrs' blood."*

He had also said:

> *"The monsoon was disadvantageous to us. Our roads were submerged. The river traffic had to be against the current; against this, the enemy had first-class roads. Our only chance was to take Imphal before the rains started, and we would have succeeded if we had more air support and if the enemy forces in Imphal had no special orders to make a stand to the last man."*

He elaborated that they should have started the campaign in January; that their timing was wrong. In that case, we could have taken Tiddim, Pallel and Kohima a little easily. The rain spoiled our game as we had to postpone our assault on Kohima. Our enemy had sent mechanized divisions, and so, they were able to retake Kohima-Imphal road.

Allies' indiscriminate bombing at Lotpaching (a hillock) had frustrated INA's efforts to advance on the state Capital. Wasn't INA's performance a lot of ifs and buts story? Was it not a case of poor planning and inefficient leadership? These questions along with several others need more researching than commenting upon.

As is well known, Bose had organized those surrendered lot of the British Army, mostly desperate Indians—including Manipuris and war refugees—into the Indian National Army, (Azad Hind Fouz) in Singapore just to be able to build up a core fighting force to throw the British out of India. The Japanese Army and the INA attempted to march to Delhi through Burma, Manipur, the Naga Hills and Assam—where they got stuck against the better-organized and better-serviced allied forces. They were distraught that despite great battles of Imphal, Kohima, Bishnupur, Kakching, Pallel, Moreh, Tamu et cetera, the dream of moving to Delhi was lost forever. Thousands got killed while many others perished through hunger and disease in the jungles, villages and on roadsides of the inhospitable terrain.

Reprocessed Army

It was a terrible end of a ***'reprocessed army'*** theoretically designed for a gigantic objectivity. Its composition, training and equipment possibly didn't match its grand objectives.

Since July 1944, allies had begun to drive the INA and Japanese from the Naga Hills, Manipur and Burma, and regained the territories lost earlier. In the meantime, the American onslaught, prior to use of atom bombing, was equally successful in driving out the Japanese occupants of the Pacific Islands, Philippines, Okinawa etc.

An army of volunteers (or even that of mercenaries) is always superior to the one that is composed of surrendered soldiers—re-recruited under coercion and/or threat. INA assembled in Singapore by one Major Mohan Singh as per the wishes of Japanese, and his own aversion to the British—his former benefactors—was indeed a reprocessed force. Mohan Singh employed fair and not-so-fair means to entice surrendered British Army soldiers kept in the Changi POWs camp—45,000 in number. Retraining a trained soldier (i.e. to do a different job or do a job in a different manner) is as difficult as retraining a trained but lost bull (who looks for his freedom). Normally, guerrilla armies are super tenacious because they consist of volunteers who are intensely committed to a job or a mission.

Last Hope of the Great Patriot

Subhash Bose's philosophical attachment to the Soviet Union was possibly very deep. Even after the defeat of INA in the battlefields of Manipur and Nagaland, he had for some time holed himself with the INA's top brass somewhere in Burma. And as late as August 14, 1945, he issued his last order… hoping to fight for the freedom of his motherland, perhaps with Russian help. And eventually, he attempted to go to USSR via Manchuria. The fateful flight failed him.

Netaji might have lost the war, but he won his countrymen's hearts. His heart-rending ***'Jai Hind'—the INA logo***—became the widely-accepted form of greetings in the Indian Army, the political gentry and even the rural populace in post-1947 India. INA's theme-song ***'Kadam Kadam Barhaye Ja'*** became another martial rendition of the Indian Army band, and it so movingly recited its own classic creation, ***'Saarey Jahan Se Achcha…***…' that both INA and Netaji became deeply enshrined in the living memory of the country, and were to remain so forever.

INA Trials: A Great Glory to Netaji

INA soldiers and officers who surrendered on the Indo-Burma front, or were captured, were transported to India and lodged at locations scattered in Bengal, Maharashtra, in and around Delhi, and also in Punjab and Sindhi. From the 43,000 strong INA, about 16,000 fighters were taken prisoners and after screening, only 12,000 were transported to India.

Between November 1945 and May 1946, several trials were held at the Red Fort. The first of these trials pertained to a joint court martial of senior INA officers—Col. Prem Sahgal, Col. Gurbaksh Singh Dhillon and Maj. Gen. Shah Nawaz Khan—who were officers of the British Indian army before they were taken prisoners by the Japanese in operations of Malaya, Singapore and Burma. They, along with a large number of surrendered British troops and numerous volunteers influenced by the objectivity of the free India's army, had joined the INA in 1942, when it was assembled by Mohan Singh and Rash Behari Bose with Japanese support and guidance. Within months of its birth, differences between its commanders and their Japanese benefactors led to its disbanding. It was the 2nd avatar of INA; an earlier one was attempted in Germany.

In 1943, soon after on his entry into the eastern sector of the Great War, Subhash Chandra Bose reactivated the INA and assumed its overall command. He energized it to a level that it battled the British Indian Army and Commonwealth forces, along with the Nipponese troops. As stated earlier, they had significant initial success but were defeated by the allied forces in battle of Imphal and Kohima. During 1944 and 1945, in addition to several minor ones, INA in association with the Japanese fought significant battles at Pokoku and Mandalay, and finally in Kohima and Imphal. Dwindling fortunes of Japan, shortage of supplies, emboldened surge of the allied forces, allied air superiority and heavy monsoon led to defeat of the INA.

While soldiers and some officials of INA surrendered or were captured, Bose with his key associates escaped to avoid arrest and/or for furthering their unfinished agenda of freeing India from British imperialists.

In the first joint trial, INA's key officers were charged with waging war against the King Emperor, and the charges included that of treason, torture, murder and abetment of murder et cetera. Jawaharlal Nehru, Bhulabhai Desai, Kailashnath Katju, Asaf Ali and some other prominent lawyers of the independence era defended those who faced the court martial under various provisions of the military law, constitutional law, and international law. They did a very competent job.

The defense lawyers' arguments, particularly those of Nehru, were hugely forceful and proved highly effective on grounds of patriotism and desire for freeing Mother India.

The INA trials that occurred just a year or so before the British packed their bags generated a massive storm of interest, sympathy and protest agitations all over India. The main defendants of the first trial were sentenced to deportation for life, which caused a storm of protests—a sort of widespread trans-India uprising. There was no newspaper or periodical that didn't front-page the trial proceedings, morning after morning. Calcutta, Delhi and numerous other major and minor cities/ towns witnessed innumerable protest marches and agitations. Raising slogans in favour of INA and Bose became a passion for one and all. The author himself recollects having heard and raised such slogans.

The pro-INA patriotic surge reached even the most remote villages in all corners of India. For the purpose, INC and Muslim League momentarily buried their political differences and collectively denounced the trials with full vigour. Numerous units of the British Indian Army and Navy, still fresh from having witnessed horrors of the WW II, mutinied or were at the verge of it, turning administrators of the Raj nervous.

Compelled by the British inability of dealing with the emerging challenge, a good sense prevailed and the then Army Chief, Claude Anchinleck, recommended to the Viceroy of India for commuting the sentences awarded to INA combatants who were held in Raj's custody.

They all walked free as glorious combatants of free India.

Possibly, Bose at the time of his separation from his combatants couldn't fathom what environment of agitation and chaos that the presence of his imprisoned INA soldiers was to create in India, which already was passing through a final phase of its struggle for independence from the British. Most likely, Bose's advisors prevailed upon him to escape and eventually mount outside pressure on the victorious British to treat the INA prisoners leniently.

His Indian contacts and admirers, particularly those from the '***Forward Bloc***' and also those in Congress, for unknown reasons, didn't do a good job of keeping him well-posted about the unprecedented ground-swell of sympathy that he and his INA soldiers had come to command all over India. Irrespective of political and religious divide, every Indian was proud of them—and Bose, at that moment, had become the greatest national hero.

Bose's Greatest Mistake

Not surrendering with his INA soldiers and their commanders was decidedly the greatest mistake committed by the great Indian revolutionary. British couldn't have afforded to hang him as the Raj was struggling with its last breaths. They were dead-scared of Indian soldiers, of the large Indian army revolting and lynching all those with white skin and their supporters. Was Bose not aware of the fact that the Great War had weakened the British beyond recovery, and that their capacity to retain colonies was hugely compromised? He was expected to have known the great ground-swell of sympathy that INA had secured in hearts and minds of the Indian public. What propelled him to make an erroneous decision hasn't been clarified by any one of his numerous biographers, fans and family members.

Bose, indeed, missed the golden opportunity of witnessing his own glory skyrocketing on the Independent India's newly emerging horizons. Had he been with his soldiers during these trials, nothing could have stopped him from rising to claim the top job when, just a few months later, India attained independence.

Bose: A Persona of Tense Relationships

Bose was endowed with a strong personality, sharp intellect and bold response which often propelled him to being perceived as '***authoritarian***

and non-compromising'. These are undesirable characteristics in a politician if he or she is to succeed in a long and arduous career. This, most likely, was the reason that for almost over one-and-a-half decade that he spent in the Congress party, his relationship with Mahatma Gandhi and even with some other key leaders of this freedom struggle spearheading outfit, was often tense. He didn't seem to possess skills, or more precisely, the patience and malleability of a durable politician.

Bose: A Self-appointed Diplomat

After his dramatic escape to Europe in 1941, until tragic and/or mysterious end in August 1945, Bose had to metamorphose himself into the role of a diplomat in a conflict-intense environment. He was a **'self-appointed'** diplomat representing India's interests. He had to do the difficult job of hard-selling himself and his revolutionary concept of freeing India from British rule, with borrowed help and/or resources. By powers whose help he sought or demanded, his own constituency back home in India wasn't perceived as being a very strong one. His ***'Forward Bloc'*** wasn't doing any impressive job, non-violently and/or violently.

It hadn't grown into an impressive militant force that could be relied upon by outside powers for serving as a base for any larger campaign aimed at freeing India. Bose advocated military means for pushing the British rulers out of India without himself being a military-man. His skills and experience were probably seen deficient for the challenging mission. These, amongst others, were probably the reasons that he wasn't taken seriously, at least initially, by various anti-British powers.

Despite the limitations, he vigorously engaged himself in the difficult job of diplomacy all through the critical years of WW II. In Italy, Germany, Soviet Union and Japan, he dealt with socialists, communists and fascists at various levels—right from ambassadors, generals, ministers, and sometimes, even with the dictators themselves. Although the success rate of his unique endeavour wasn't bad, the relations with benefactors in Germany, Soviet Union and Japan continued to be tense. They weren't ever so smooth that he could take independent decisions and/or demand situation altering resources.

As a military man and as the leader of the legendry INA, his success at India's eastern borders was outstanding. His combatants and commanders loved and respected him. But the way the legendry INA disintegrated when Japanese lost the war against allied assault didn't speak highly of the great leader's military organizational skills. He and his commanders weren't able to develop a fighting infrastructure that could make an independent stand and continue with its goal even for a few more weeks or months without Japanese support. He exhibited no skills of perseverance as the same were so much visible in case of Fidel Castro of Cuba, or Mao Zedong of China.

And was putting all the eggs in the Japanese basket right? This issue hasn't been analyzed by researchers and biographers who took interest in Bose and INA in the past over seven decades.

Obviously, there was no plan B to go into forests and turn remnants of the INA into a massive guerilla warfare challenge. Forested and hilly terrain on the Indo-Burma border and the famous Naga Hills was just right for the purpose. Post-independence, Naga rebels and several other militant outfits did it so efficiently for long decades.

Was Bose a fair weather fighter? Though doubts exist but nothing has been said with certainty.

Some analysts have, however, commented that Bose was a ***'conference room warrior'***. But whatsoever deficiencies he suffered with, Bose was a great motivator of people, soldiers as well as civilians.

Bose: A Perpetual Non-conformist

Revolutionaries aren't made for conformity. By basic understanding, they are deviations from the normal and Bose, too, fully fitted the frame of non-conformity. In life, through multilateral deviations and in death, vide the huge mystery and myth that were generated, he proved superbly true to the non-conformist genre of revolutionaries.

- Subhash was a difficult child. The lack of individual care and love that a middle child in a large family of 11 siblings is bound to suffer caused him, as per his own admission, to have hated his parents. He became a rebel at an early age.

- In missionary schools that he attended as a young boy, he wasn't comfortable with his European teachers. Their emphasis on European culture and Bible studies anguished him a great deal.
- As a young student at Presidency College in Calcutta, he fell into a group of seditious students, and was expelled.
- He loved the charisma of military but failed in his attempts to get selected for entry into the British Indian Army.
- His political life in 2nd and 3rd decades of the 20th century was full of contradictions and non-conformity. He joined the Indian National Congress as prompted by his mentor CR Das, but soon caused discord in the organization on account of his advocacy of violent approach to the struggle for independence... which went against the basic Gandhian ideology. He wanted speed and usage of force for pushing the British imperialists out of India. He was elected as Congress president in 1938, but was soon suspended due to controversies that he courted relentlessly.
- With like-minded leftists in the Congress itself, he subsequently founded ***'Forward Bloc'*** as a pressure group but without enabling it to grow to politically decisive strengths. In early 1941, he escaped from house arrest for trying his luck with the then dominant communists and fascists forces of Europe. There too, he ran into numerous controversies and was disillusioned with the German fascists with regard to their inability either to defeat the allied powers or assist his group to make any meaningful dent in pushing the British out of India.
- Non-conformist undoubtedly, Bose hadn't learnt to give up to the last. And pursuing his objectivity with support of his benefactor fascists, he secretly moved to the East Asian theater of war, which then was dominated by the Japanese. There, with Singapore as headquarters, he revived the INA into its 3rd version with material and strategic support from the massive Japanese war machine.
- Through the INA and in company of the Nipponese Army, he gave a good fight to the British and Commonwealth forces in Burma, and on the Indo-Burma borders. In 1945, heavily bombed by the allies, Japanese lost will to continue the fight, and with it, INA lost the cause of its existence too. Crushing

reverses at Kohima and Imphal saw the INA disintegrated; more than half of its combatants abandoned the operations and, wounded and hungry, they melted into the masses in Burma and Malaysia. Over 16, 000 surrendered to the British and, after screening by the captors, about 12, 000 were transported to India.

- Bose and some of his close associates, supposedly as per their own choice or under duress from Japanese, elected to move to the company of the retreating Nipponese forces.
- In death, Bose fuelled more controversies than the ones that were created during his whole revolutionary career. Even on passage of seven decades since his death or disappearance on 18th August in 1945, Bose continues to confuse his family members, admirers and also the politicians of independent India— all of who want to grab his legacy for electoral interests.

Bose: Early Sparks of Rebellion

Subhash was born on January 23, 1897 as a middle child (6th amongst 11 siblings), in a well-known family headed by lawyer Jankinath Bose. The family was settled in Cuttack, a small town in Eastern India. Modern psychologists tend to deduce that being at the center of a large group of children, the young Subhash possibly suffered neglect and lack of attention, resulting in a paucity of love. It is feared that his emotional insecurities resulting from being a middle male child in a large family subsequently got compounded due to rigidity of Christian missionary schooling, where excessive attention on Bible studies and discipline acted as a trigger. The inherent bigotry of the system and its non-Indian character stunned the young mind, eventually igniting flames of patriotism on one hand, and hatred for the British, on the other.

> *"Subhash remembered being awed by his parents, and he always desired a closer relationship with them. The lack of parental love in his large family taught Subhash the importance of compatibility, although that lack limited both his development as an individual, and any sense of confidence."*[1]
>
> "*I used to feel like a thoroughly insignificant being,*"[2] Subhash wrote as an adult.

He found missionary education with its English medium quite daunting, and missionary educators' avoidance of enabling local children to deal with social problems in colonial environment coupled with frequent spankings for minor acts of misbehavior, or lack of good manners, compounded adjustment and learning challenges faced by the children. Young Bose not only faced such situations, but vigorously reacted to them.

Seeds of revolt so germinating subsequently matured into a full blast of revolutionary built-up.

Upwardly mobile English educated people, the Bengali babus in particular, pushed their children to suffer missionary education that eventually alienated them from Indian culture, sartorial and dietary habits, and even religion. Young Bose didn't appreciate the blind copying of the West by most of the educated Indians of his time. Although in later period of his life Bose had became famous as a Westernized politician of Asia, he never forgot that he belonged to the Bose clan—a Khatriya or warrior community of India. Over centuries, the Bose community of Bengal had excelled first in military services, and then as politicians and writers. Subhash felt obliged to maintain the tradition of the community, and until the end, never felt comfortable fully merging into the Western culture. The Indian-ness and ***'Mother India'***, both were dear to him.

During his school years, young Subhash worked hard with the purpose of avoidance of failure, and eventually entered university. Along with studies, he read through numerous books on Hindu philosophy and practiced yoga and meditation. As a young boy, Bose wasn't athletic but attractively plump.

The devastating partition of Bengal in 1905 had inflamed the already active Indian nationalism. The flames continued to coincide with the adolescent years of Subhash Bose. He entered college when flames of patriotism were glowing impressively, and the young Bose couldn't remain untouched by the same.

Although the adolescent Bose reacted sympathetically to those who opposed the partition of Bengal and the news related to them, his political baptism occurred only after he entered the Presidency College. Living away from home granted him new freedom. And this son of a lawyer, a member of the provincial gentry, learned ways of the world in Calcutta—the center of Bengali intellectualism and patriotism at that time. The college exposure emboldened him, and now, he didn't even hesitate rebelling against his parents.

Tracking Subhash's emerging revolting nature, Marshal J Getz[1] quoted as under from a history source:

> *"I had no hesitation in disobeying them," he wrote, "because by the time I believed....that revolt is necessary for self-fulfillment—that when a child is born, it's very cry is a revolt against the bondage in which it finds itself."*

Foundation of Bose's personality as a militant revolutionary was laid during his Presidency days. By default, he reportedly fell into a group of seditious students who advocated use of violence as a means for liberating India. Although he disagreed with them and advocated that achievement of India's freedom shall depend upon a 'process of natural reconstruction', the British intelligence noted his presence with the group and then onwards kept a watch on him.

Now, Bose took greater interest in politics than studies, and advocated an organized movement, using force as the last resort. These group of rowdies even attacked their conservative British professors, and Bose got entangled into these activities which enhanced his revolutionary and trouble genesis potential in eyes of the Raj's administrators. On account of one such assault, Bose got expelled from college in 1916.

Subhash, propelled by his militant nationalism, attempted to join the British Indian Army but was rejected. Subsequently, his efforts to rejoin the Presidency College too were unsuccessful because of his tainted record. Frustrated, he then joined the Scottish Church College in Calcutta. There, he joined the officers' training unit of Bengali cadets called the ***'Indian Defense Force'.***

Here, he concentrated on studies, keeping politics in background for the time being. He graduated in 1919 with a Bachelor of Arts degree.

CHAPTER 4

POLITICAL UPBRINGING OF BOSE

Unwarranted Partition of Bengal

Political personality of Bose was shaped substantially in the chaotic environment erupting out of the post-Bengal partition years (1905 to 1920), which caused multilateral social, cultural, political and economic eruptions in the Bengali society—especially amongst its intellectuals and business classes. Rumblings of the WW I had compounded these currents of upheavals as Raj's administration looked unequal of dealing with lootings, robberies, and bomb-blasts resorted to by anguished and dissatisfied local population.

Unhappiness against the unwarranted partition of the state of Bengal had fuelled spurting of Swadeshi movement. In 1906, Congress meeting in Calcutta, under its famed statesmen-publisher Dadabhai Naoroji, gave the emerging Swaraj movement its official beginning. At that time, Bose was too young to be drawn into the movement but its post WW I manifestations took the young revolutionary into its massive folds.

At that time, the concept of Swaraj or self-rule didn't imply independence; it rather meant more of an opportunity for Indians to control domestic affairs of the colony. However, for active nationalists, it meant the first step towards eventual freedom. And in due course, attention shifted from local problems and discontent of Bengal to injustices being perpetrated all over the country by the British occupiers.

Winds of Swadeshi and Swaraj

In the post WW I period, winds of Swadeshi and Swaraj led to beginning of local industrialization; a number of jute mills, textile units and low technology works like soap making flooded the local industrial scene. Bose never missed importance of small businesses and new industries. He was conscious of the fact that Japan and Germany had grown on the back of industrial growth. Russian revolution and peasants' movement, too, influenced Indian intellectuals; but communism never really took deep roots in the Indian political scenario. Swadeshi hurt British businesses a great deal, and Raj retaliated by creating all possible impediments in path of local entrepreneurs. Despite problems and setbacks, the movement lingered on—later to be picked up vigorously by Mahatma Gandhi and his associates. In decades of 1930s and 40s, it became a massive movement.

Bose Finds a Soul-mate

Subhash Bose entered the post WW I political scene in Bengal with interest of a great learner; he found that while the general population longed for '**home-rule**', the organized violence wasn't yet seen as an effective vehicle of change. Established businesses were in a mood to support the anti-Raj movement. In 1923, CR Das, a High Court lawyer and Gandhi's lieutenant, became president of the increasingly influential All India Trade Union Congress. Bose came under Das' influence; he actually found a soul-mate in the great Bengali freedom fighter.

Kisan movements and labour unions were seen by the British imperialists as the first cadre-based associations of Raj opponents and socialists. Bose was attracted to such developments. Das and Bose collectively entered into publishing a liberal paper called ***'Forward'***. During the association, Das convinced the young Bose to participate in the Gandhian civil disobedience movement.

Key Influences on Bose

In early years, Lenin and Russian revolution, Lok Manya Tilak, Mahatma Gandhi, Giuseppe Garibaldi of Italy, and Joan d'Arc of France influenced the young Bose. While in his 30s (and afterwards), Mussolini and Hitler's fascism, authoritarianism of Stalin of Russia and, in the final run, the Nipponese fascism had great impact on the maturing personality of the great Indian revolutionary.

Bal Gangadhar Tilak: *Swaraj* was his slogan, and it remained the slogan of most of the freedom fighters till the country became free in August 1947.

He was described as the ***'Father of the Indian Unrest'*** by the British. He was the founder of the radical Indian consciousness.

Tilak had developed an alliance with Congress leaders of his time, prominently with Bipin Chandra Pal, Lala Lajpat Rai, Aurobindo Ghose, Chidambaram Pillai and MA Jinnah. Gopal Krishna Gokhle, a moderate, headed the opposite faction of Congress that insisted on non-violent methods of agitation against the British Raj. Gandhi came to India in 1915 and Tilak died in 1920, but the latter strongly differed with the total *ahimsa* as a political tool. Tilak advocated use of force, and that part of the first great revolutionary of India attracted young Bose the most.

In his written works Tilak referred to ***"Bhagavad Gita"*** to stress that no blame could be attached to anyone who killed an oppressor without any thought of reward.

Encouraged by his views, some of his admirers took to violence and killed some British officials, and the Raj administration blamed Tilak for spreading violence and shielding culprits. He was jailed several times in his over-three-decades of active political career.

In a 1908 case related to the violent act committed by two of Tilak's associates, while being sentenced and on being asked by the judge whether he had anything to say, Tilak had said:

All that I wish to say is that in spite of the verdict of the jury, I still maintain that I am innocent. There are higher powers that rule the destinies of men and nations; and I think it may be the will of Providence that the cause I represent may be benefited more by my suffering than by my pen and tongue.

Tilak, through his publication called '***Keshri***' supported his followers and revolutionaries and often called for immediate Swaraj.

Bose didn't have time to personally interact with Tilak as he joined Congress only in 1923 on CR Das' persuasion. And by that time, Tilak had left this world. But the revolutionary trail lit by him always attracted Bose.

Joan d'Arc: She was a French peasant girl who believing that she had heard divine voice led the French armies which defeated the British in 1429 and 1430 during the historic 100 years' war. She was captured and handed over to the English who burned her at the stake—claiming that she promoted witchcraft and heresy.

She was canonized in 1920, and has been a great inspiration to many. And young Bose, too, was greatly inspired by her heroic deeds.

Giuseppe Garibaldi: Giuseppe Garibaldi was an Italian general and politician, and a nationalist who played a large role in the history of Italy. He is considered, with Camillo Cavour, Victor Emmanuel II and Giuseppe Mazzini, as one of Italy's '***Fathers of the Fatherland***'.

He was born in 1807 in Nice, then in France. Garibaldi was a central figure in the Italian Risorgimento since outstanding personalities of his time, such as Victor Higo, Alexander Dumas and George Sand, admired him because he personally commanded and fought in many military campaigns that led eventually to the unification of Italy. He was appointed as general by the provisional government of Milan in 1848. As General of the Roman Republic, he led the expedition of thousands on behalf of, and with the consent of Victor Emmanuel II.

He has been called '***Hero of Two Worlds***' because of his military enterprises in Brazil, Uruguay and Europe. These earned him a considerable reputation in Italy and abroad, aided by exceptional international media coverage at the time. Red shirts, as per popular telling, were the dress of his co-fighters. He was master of guerilla wars and could fight, win or retreat with ease.

Bose was influenced by his tenacity and war methodology. In personal habits, he was a simple man. But developments during the last days of

INA's campaign against the allied forces at the Indo-Burma border didn't show that the Garibaldi character had any lasting impact on Subhash Bose.

Russian Revolution: Just towards end of WW I, Russia was overtaken by a frenzy of civil unrests called revolutions.

The Russian Revolution is the collective term for a pair of revolutions in 1917, which dismantled the Tsarist autocracy and led to the eventual rise of the Soviet Union.

The conflict occurred between public combatants and Russian provisional government.

People were unhappy with food shortages, corruption and the incompetency and insensitivity of the rulers, and the bureaucracy that managed the states.

In 1917, two revolutions swept through Russia, ending centuries of imperial rule and setting in motion a series of political and social changes that led to the formation of the Soviet Union. In March, growing civil unrest coupled with chronic food shortages, erupted into open revolt—forcing the abdication of Nicholas II (1868-1918), the last Russian Czar. Just months later, the newly-installed provisional government was itself overthrown by the more radical Bolsheviks, led by Vladimir Lenin (1870-1924).

Czar Nicholas II government by the year 1917 had lost faith of the people as corruption was rampant; the state was insensitive to miseries of people and the Russian economy was rotting. And seeing no way out, Nicholas repeatedly dissolved the Duma, the Russian parliament. Russia's disastrous involvement in the WW I (1914-18) was the most defining event. The Imperial Russia was militarily no match to an industrialized Germany, and hence, Russian casualties were much greater than those sustained by any nation in the Great War. Additionally, the economy was hopelessly disrupted by the costly war effort and, as a result, the frustrated moderates joined Russian radical elements in calling for the overthrow of the Czar too.

After Czar Nicholas II and his family were executed by the Bolshevik forces, their bodies were badly mutilated as a result of anger expression. The remains were discovered and exhumed only in the late 1970s near Yekaterinburg, Russia, and eventually identified through DNA testing.

In February, demonstrators clamouring for bread took to the streets in the Russian capital of Petrograd (now St. Petersburg), and went uncontrolled. Supported by huge crowds of striking industrial workers, the emboldened protesters clashed with police and refused to leave the streets. By March, the strike spread among all of Petrograd's workers, and irate mobs destroyed police stations. Several factories elected their own deputies to the Petrograd Soviet, or council of workers' committees, following the model devised during the 1905 revolution.

Troops from the Petrograd army garrison were called out to quell the uprising. In some encounters, regiments opened fire, killing demonstrators. But the protesters kept to the streets and the troops began to waver. That day, Nicholas again dissolved the Duma. On March 12, the revolution triumphed when almost all the regiments of the Petrograd garrison defected to the cause of the demonstrators. The soldiers subsequently formed committees that elected deputies to the Petrograd Soviet.

As a consequence, the imperial government resigned, and the Duma formed a provisional government that peacefully joined with the Petrograd Soviet for control of the revolution.

Soon, the order was established and the demonstrators started to behave. And next day i.e. March 15, Czar Nicholas II abdicated the throne in favour of his brother Michael (1878-1918), whose refusal of the crown brought an end to the Czarist autocracy.

After the February Revolution, power was shared between the weak provisional government and the Petrograd Soviet. Then, on October 24 and 25, the leftist revolutionaries led by Bolshevik party leader Vladimir Lenin launched a nearly bloodless coup d'état against the provisional government. The Bolsheviks and their allies occupied government buildings and other strategic locations in Petrograd, and soon formed a new government with Lenin as its head.

Thus, Lenin became the virtual dictator of the first Marxist state in the world. His government made peace with Germany, nationalized industries and distributed land. Lenin skillfully crushed the anti-Bolshevik forces and finally formed the Union of Soviet Socialist Republics (USSR). It was a great achievement.

Bengali intellectuals were greatly influenced by the integrative achievements of Lenin, which in a strong manner, demonstrated the power of workers. Collective farms were introduced and a great industrial development took place, elevating the Soviet Union to superpower status within just over two decades.

Bose was naturally influenced by the march of communism, industrial development and the international power display of the first great socialist nation.

Axis Powers: The three important constituents in the Axis alliance were Germany, Italy and Japan. They had collectively recognized German domination over most of continental Europe; Italian domination over the Mediterranean states was accepted, and Japanese were to dominate over East Asia and the Pacific. On the opposite, the Allied Powers were led by Great Britain and the United States; Russia was initially non-committal, but after being attacked by Germany, it joined the Allies by default.

The Axis partners, unlike the Allies, never institutionalized command and control of the war machinery and foreign policy instruments: they had two common interests:

1) Territorial expansion and foundation of empires based on military conquests, and the overthrow of the post-World War I international order;
2) The destruction and/or neutralization of Soviet Communism.

In November 1936, Germany and Italy, reflecting their common interests in destabilizing the European order, announced a Rome-Berlin Axis one week after signing a treaty of friendship. And about a month after in November 25, 1936, Nazi Germany and Imperial Japan signed the so-called "**Anti-Comintern Pact**" directed at the Soviet Union. Italy joined the Anti-Comintern Pact in November 1937.

Subhash Bose was not only aware of these developments, but saw a lot of scope for the Indian revolutionary elements to benefit from the same.

Further, on May 22, 1939, Germany and Italy signed the so-called "***Pact of Steel***", formalizing the Axis alliance with military provisions. Finally, on September 27, 1940, Germany, Italy and Japan signed the Tripartite Pact, which became known as the Axis Alliance.

Subsequently, Hungary and some Balkan states too joined the Axis powers.

Bose was greatly influenced with the Axis powers' energy and resources; their industrial development had especially influenced him a great deal. In mid 1930s, Bose visited Italy as well as Germany and requested the two dictators—Benito Mussolini of Italy and Adolf Hitler of Germany—to help him free India from the British imperialistic control through usage of military means. He was impressed with the former a great deal and gave him a copy of his book, an autobiography. Hitler, on the other hand, wasn't that forthcoming because the great dictator didn't want to start a process of colonized countries gaining freedom. Germany had several of its own colonies to begin with.

Even otherwise, the great dictator thought very poorly of Asians, Africans and other races, except the European Aryans. And his knowledge of India and Indians was rudimentary in nature, which is clearly reflected in his controversial book titled '***Mien Kemp***'.

Despite his unsuccessful interactions with the two great dictators of Europe, Bose didn't give up on possibilities of help from them in his great mission. When the WW II skirmishes commenced in 1939, Bose's admiration of the two dictators swelled a great deal. And on his escape from house arrest in early 1941, through Russia, he landed in Germany.

CHAPTER 5

MYSTERY OF BOSE'S DEATH AND DISAPPEARANCE

Bose's death in a plane crash at Taipei in Taiwan (then called Formosa) on August 18, 1945 is a well-documented event, yet the mystery or stories of his disappearance into Manchuria, Russia, and/or Central Asia—and then the story of the great revolutionary living an ascetic life in some places in India—have been planted and nurtured assiduously by interested political and non-political elements. These elements were primarily Indian, and more specifically from Bengali community. The large Bose family, its subsequent generations, their friends and relatives and disgruntled politicians, over the 70 odd years, vied with each other—some for gathering attention and a few others for pecuniary social and political gains. They made sure that the story of Bose that had huge emotional connotations stayed ever-fresh. Frequent statements about Nehru-Gandhi family's anti-Bose sentiments or intentions were turned into news stories by the hungry press. To his credit, Bose, all through the decades, remained a good line for stories—media reports, visual and/or print, were lapped up by the public and the trend goes on unabated.

Forward Bloc elements, which missed the opportunity of rising to political power and ruling India, dreamt of their hero returning home after the 1945 disastrous events at Kohina and Imphal, and were ever-ready to grab every floating straw related to Bose. During election times, they worked into frenzy as initially the Congress and then communists of varied hues didn't allow them to grab political power in West Bengal. They were never an impressive force on the political canvas in India even during Bose's time; they couldn't be an effective alternative either to Congress or Muslim League. Had the situation been different, the need for Bose to escape to Europe for gathering help to push the perpetrators of Raj out of India wouldn't have been that compelling.

History would have been different if Bose wasn't in too much of a hurry or had a little patience to work with the dominant forces striving for independence of India.

Three Commissions and the Non-truth

There has been persistent denial of the well-documented truth of Bose's death in a plane crash in August 1945 when, with help of his Japanese benefactors, he attempted to escape the dragnet of the allied powers. He possibly didn't think that the victorious British would treat him fairly, or the Japanese authorities didn't want a great ally like Bose to fall into allied powers' hands.

Shah Nawaz Committee

In 1956, the Government of India constituted a committee to look into the circumstances around death and/or disappearance of Bose, with Shah Nawaz Khan as the head. The committee included Bose's elder brother Suresh Chandra Bose as well. The Committee began its work in April 1956, and concluded four months later when two out of the three members (excluding Suresh Chandra Bose) firmly opined that on August 18, 1945, Bose had died in the airplane crash at an airbase called Taihoku (Japanese for Taipei) in Taiwan (earlier called Formosa). They stated that his ashes were kept in a Japanese temple and should be reinstated to India.

Suresh Chandra Bose, in his 181-page repetitive document, rigorously strived to reject all available documents and evidences related to the plane crash that killed Subhash. It seemed that his conclusions were preconceived and carried the objectivity of keeping the story of the great leader's missing alive and well-fuelled. The major principle for his dealing with the evidences was:

That if two or more stories by witnesses had any discrepancies or variation between them, then the whole testimony of the witnesses involved was discredited and assumed to be false. Using this principle, Suresh Bose was able to conclude that there was no crash and that his brother lived somewhere in disguise. Another unrealistic assumption that Subhash Bose was a super-human, and hence could not die before India became independent, continued to be the main theme of some of his relatives and admirers. Therefore, as per the myth so assiduously fuelled, the great hero didn't die in the plane crash that had taken place on August 18, 1945.

Shah Nawaz Khan, a captain in the British Indian Army, saw action against the Nipponese Army in the eastern region where he was taken prisoner in 1942. As a POW in Singapore, he was greatly impressed by speeches of Bose. He saw true India and its potential as a free country through the eyes of Bose. He joined INA in 1943 and rose to command a division. He fought at Kohima and Imphal, where for a short period; INA held these areas under over all control of the Japanese. In 1945, he along with numerous other senior combatants of INA fell into the lap of the victorious British. In 1945/46, he along with several of his INA colleagues faced trials at the Red Fort. Imbalanced by widespread protests, agitations and even mutinies in the British Indian Army, especially navy, the authorities of Raj couldn't carry out the punishment that was awarded to INA defendants.

Impressed by Gandhian thoughts of non-violence, he joined Congress and later became a minister in independent India's cabinet. He was elected to Parliament several times, and headed different ministries in the Central government.

Khosla Commission

Responding to continued stories and/or rumours about Subhash Bose—that he was roaming around somewhere in Northern plains—in 1970, Justice Khosla was assigned the job of unearthing the truth. After long investigations, he suggested that motives of many of the Bose-related story-purveyors were less than altruistic. Some, he said, had clearly been driven by political goals or simply wanted to call attention to themselves. His patience in listening to some tales was surely remarkable. What could he, or anyone, have thought as he listened to the testimony of one PM Karapurkar, agent of the Central Bank of India at Sholapur, who claimed that he regularly received direct messages from Bose by tuning his body like a radio receiving apparatus?

Several of Bose's fans and family members felt that the Khosla Commission was biased against them as it took their submissions and claims only with a pinch of salt. They were disappointed with its conclusion that the great revolutionary had indeed died in the plane crash.

Mukherjee Commission

In 1999, following a court order, the Indian government appointed a retired Supreme Court judge named M.K. Mukherjee to probe the death and/or disappearance of Bose. The commission perused hundreds of files on Bose's death drawn from several countries and also visited Japan, Russia and Taiwan.

Rejecting oral accounts which were in favour of the plane crash, the commission doggedly concluded that those accounts could not be relied upon; that there was a secret plan to ensure Bose's safe passage to Russia with the knowledge of Japanese authorities and Habibur Rahman. The commission also observed that the ashes kept at the Renkoji temple reported to be Bose's, were of Ichiro Okura, a Japanese soldier who had died of cardiac arrest.

What were Habibur Rahman and other eye witnesses' objective to be part of the presumed conspiracy? It wasn't clarified a bit. What stopped Bose from contacting Government of India, or his family and professional friends for so many years if he lived, or roamed around in Russia, Central Asia or in North India? The issue wasn't dealt with diligently by the learned Justice.

Was Bose such a weakling that he would be scared of telephoning or writing to even one person, politician or otherwise? Was Bose so generous that he would let Nehru-Gandhi combine to rule unhindered for so many years? None of such clarifications were forthcoming.

The Mukherjee Commission submitted its report on November 8, 2005. The report was tabled in the Indian Parliament on May 17, 2006. The Indian Government rejected the findings of the commission without assigning any reason. Some members of the Bose family welcomed the government's decision while others opposed it. But Mukherjee stood by his report and said that he was happy with whatever he had done, and that the present day Indian government may find it difficult to accept it.

The Mukherjee Commission, after consuming six long years and spending a lot of public money, further confused the issue. It was, most probably, its unstated objective to keep the Bose myth alive for the benefit of some anti-Congress political elements that had gained strength in several states. They wanted to continue to exploit public's Bose-related sentiments.

In fact, the learned Judge wasn't in a hurry to finish his report. He would have liked to continue to enjoy the public-financed paraphernalia that went with such an investigation, for a longer time.

Bose knew that World War II would break the backbone of England's economy, and he believed that if not internally, independence could be achieved with the help of political and diplomatic relations and allies. He probably had an idea (or misconception) that Soviets will be a good friend of India, and will always be supporting it.

And the learned judge's findings, a few years later, seemed totally at variance (discussed herein a little later) with those of the UK-based website that clearly confirmed Bose's death in a plane crash.

Whatever may the actual truth be, Subhash Chandra Bose was one of the greatest leaders of India's independence struggle—starting as a radical wing of INC and later becoming a true legend respected by one and all, and lovingly called Netaji.

Netaji's Cremation Records

In January 2016, a London-based website said to have been set up with the purpose of unveiling the death/or disappearance mystery of Subhash Chandra Bose, based on the evidence given by a Taiwanese official who claimed that he had, in fact, prepared Bose's dead body for cremation after the great Indian's death in a plane crash on August 18, 1945, clarified the relevant death records.

The clarification was said to have been unearthed from the UK foreign office's file number FC1852/6 dated 1956, which was amongst the last few Bose-related documents released by www.Bosefiles.info that was designed to establish how the great Indian revolutionary had died.

It reported:

> *"Taiwanese official Tan Ti-Ti who was in-charge of issuing cremation permits in Taipei together with that of other local officials, put to rest any controversy about the last rites performed on the Bose's body."*

For decades, controversies had mystified events related to the death/ or disappearance of Subhash Bose despite the Government of India having established three commissions and committees for the purpose of clarification. For over seven decades, nothing could lift clouds of misgivings and misinformation in this regard. The proof of Bose's death and cremation contained in Taiwanese police records, as per the website's report, were sent to the British Foreign Office. And in July 1956, the same were reported to have been forwarded to the Government of India by the British High Commissioner in Delhi.

British Consul General in Taiwan, on 15 May 1956, had written to the Taiwanese government for documents related to Bose's death. In response, the Taiwanese government had sent a detailed police report along with text of an interview with Tan Ti-Ti, who had conducted the last rites of the Indian leader.

A Japanese army official who had brought the body to Tan Ti-Ti was reported to have elaborated:

> *"The diseased was Bose, the Indian leader (on occasions he mentioned him as the Indian Commander) who proceeding to Tokyo on important business, was injured when his plane was involved in an accident."*

Previous day, i.e. on August 21, 1945, the same officer, according to Tan Ti-Ti, had ***"submitted the death certificate of a certain Ichiro Okura"***. It was said to have been clarified by the Taiwanese officer who gave information to the British that in absence of any family person of Bose, permission for cremation was given on basis of a death certificate from military hospital.

Thus, Bose seems to have been cremated as Ichiro Okura.

Further, Tan Ti-Ti was reported to have said that on day of cremation, the same Japanese officer was accompanied by an Indian, believed to be Col. Habibur Rahman, Bose's ADC. Rahman had survived the air crash. He had also observed that Bose's body was brought in a coffin and since it was too large to have been taken to Tokyo by available plane at that time, it was cremated there.

Next day, the Indian Colonel (Habibur Rahman) came with the same Japanese officer to collect ashes of the diseased leader. Col. Rahman's statement recorded on August 24, 1945 matched with Tan TI-Ti's account on the said website.

Now, it is to be seen how information in the Indian government files which were made public in 2016 matched or differed with obviously dependable account of the UK website.

Was Bose a War Criminal?

Government of India and the three commissions and/or committees which it established from 1956 to 1999 haven't thrown any light on this question that could settle the issue one way or the other. Many admirers of legendry Bose, who contributed to the theory that their great hero didn't die in the plane crash of August 18, 1945, continued to suspect that he disappeared in order to avoid arrest at hands of British and/or the allied powers that were victorious in the Great War of 1940s.

They also knew that their hero wasn't so obedient that he would disappear because his presence in India could not have suited the Nehru-Gandhi political combine.

He hadn't ever listened to Congress leaders when, for over 16 years in 1920s and 1930s, he was an active Congressman; he even became the president of Congress twice. Bose had gone into hiding several times before his final escape to Europe in early 1941.

But if he weren't dead in the plane crash, then the government of independent India under Nehru wasn't a strong enough roadblock for him to come here and follow his residual political and/or social agenda.

May be, he was misguided by the Japanese! Or was he ashamed of his failure at the battle field? Nothing is clear in these matters.

And neither the government nor the large Bose fraternity contributed towards causing any clarity in this regard. India's Ministry of External Affairs (MEA) and its UNP division

consistently said in response to Right to Information (RTI) queries that they had no record to suggest that Bose was a war criminal.

Allied powers' lists of war criminals have for long been in public domain, and no one has verified that his name existed there.

Then, if Bose had been alive after 1945, what kept him incognito? Such a great man could not have stayed without contacting at least one friend or relative with whom he was close in war and/or peace times. Bose was an intense social being, and it is unthinkable that he threw himself into social exclusion as a *sanyasi*.

Japanese government had no obvious objective for hiding Bose's presence. His death, as per Taiwanese records, was a verifiable mishap and there were eye witnesses—Indians as well as non-Indians. Except his Indian admirers and relatives, no one had active political and/or emotional interest in Bose's death/or disappearance mystery lasting for over seven decades. And the same people who fuelled the mystery of this great hero's death or disappearance continue to harp on the issue even in the present times.

Surprisingly the BJP and NDA elements have recently developed some active love for Bose after having been silent for so many years.

Files keeping on Bose, in light of persistent rumours of him being alive or having been sighted, was imperative for the government because:

(a) It was the Information Bureau's job to collect and assess all important developments, rumours and/or otherwise.
(b) And they also had to know why and how rumours of the great revolutionary's sighting or presence were emerging with persistent regularity.

To ignore every rumour in this context wasn't possible; and to disclose whatsoever was known, except the truth of the plane crash of August 1945, was doubly dangerous.

His admirers and relatives weren't ready to listen to anything other than a statement that he didn't die in 1945. Hence, the government could do nothing except appointing commissions and committees for the purpose of finding facts. There were political considerations in accepting and/or rejecting findings of such inquiries.

In 2015, Trinamool Congress government in West Bengal made public all Bose-related files that were in its custody. They had high expectations that some interesting skeletons would tumble out of lifting of the red tape. Nothing came out that could benefit either the state government or non-Congress politicians. They were greatly disappointed.

NDA government in New Delhi had eyes fixed at the state elections in West Bengal that fell in early half of 2016. BJP, the major component of the NDA, wanted to play the Bose card and garner Bengali sympathy as well as votes of the mercurial electorate. The target was clear to them—and they tried to work like the legendry Arjuna (fully concentrated and attentive) but failed. They had neither Brahamastra with them, nor was Lord Krishna available to advice them in difficult times.

The extended Bose family, in the middle of 2015, was treated to a high tea party at PM Narendra Modi's official 7 Race Course residence.

It was a great photo opportunity for BJP to highlight that the party held Bose in great esteem. Modi forgot that Bose, for seventeen long years, was a Congressman; that he was twice elected as the president of the then iconic party.

Modi had also met some Bose relatives in Germany when he had visited the country early in his Prime Minister-ship. As the election came near, competition between Trinamool Congress and BJP intensified for grabbing Bose-sympathetic votes.

In fact, since 1945 after the death and/or disappearance of Bose, politics always played greater or decisive role, whenever any rumour about this great revolutionary emerged. And in the near future, the fight for cornering Bose's legacy by politicians isn't going to end in a hurry.

As per Amiya Nath Bose, son of Subhash Chandra Bose's elder brother Sarat Chandra Bose, Gandhiji didn't seem to believe that Subhash Bose died in an air crash. In a letter to the then Prime Minister PV Narasimha Rao dated August 7, 1995, Amiya wrote:

> *"When Col. Habibur Rahman, who accompanied Netaji in the plane from Saigon, was released from prison, he visited Mahatma Gandhi in the Bhangi Colony in Delhi. I was present in the room when* ***Col. Habibur Rehman*** *spoke to Gandhiji about the alleged air crash at the Taikhou Airport on August 18, 1945."*

Amiya Nath was reported to have said that when Rahman left, Gandhiji told journalists assembled there:

> *"Habib is carrying out his leader's orders. I do not believe that Subhash died in any air crash."*

Gandhji was also reported to have forbidden the Bose family to perform any *shradh* for the great leader. Was the great Mahatma over-taken by emotions expressed by Amiya Nath?

One isn't sure how to take Amiya's words at face value in view of the fact that he has, all-through, been known to promote Bose's disappearance theory against the air crash that was widely believed to have killed the great revolutionary.

Amiya's assertion didn't clear the clouds of the mystery in any manner.

Serious Anxiety for the Allied World

Subhash Bose was a cause of anxiety for the British imperialists right from the day he escaped from his house arrest in early 1941. His contacts with the Axis powers were a cause of great concern. His rise in the East Asia and walking of INA into Eastern India not only unnerved the British, it had caused serious anxiety throughout the allied block.

The thought of Bose's forces grabbing India with Japanese assistance troubled them a lot. Although Bose's organization was located in Singapore, most Indians had started viewing it as a legitimate government of their oppressed homeland. Bose seemed ready to claim India for the Axis powers. And in order to face the situation, British had to draw upon American help against Bose's INA in April 1945. And finally, the Americans' dropping of atom bombs on Japan in August 1945 saved the situation for the British imperialists and their friends. They got two more years of uneasy and worrisome presence in India.

Although Bose was widely believed to have died in a mysterious air-crash two years before India's independence, his political and military activities had wholly unnerved the British. They lost faith in their capacity to hold on to India as they had grown unsure of the loyalty of Indian soldiers in their service—resulting in a crisis of confidence concerning India's struggle for freedom.

Bose: A Conference Room Revolutionary

Non-Indian historians and political commentators have often been harsh while evaluating Subhash Bose, or while making passing remarks on his role in India's fight for freedom. Indian public as well as political commentators, as expected, have been emotional in their observations on the great revolutionary.

Marshal J Getz[1] right in opening pages of his biographical work on the great Indian revolutionary observed:

"Netaji worked best in conference rooms, not the battle fields. The

> *British-educated Bose practiced statesmanship in the European tradition: understanding him, therefore requires an in-depth examination of his politics, and how events in Europe shaped his views."*

That Bose, unlike Mao Zedong and Fidel Castro, wasn't a battle-field revolutionary fighter often emerges in numerous writings/commentaries on this anti-imperialist crusader. He put immense force behind his arguments while attempting to persuade fascist regimes of Europe to help him raise a credible force for liberating India—and finally, he nearly succeeded with the Nipponese help from the East. He forcefully cajoled Indians in Europe as well as in East Asia to join him in his fight for liberation of India with the force of arms. And finally, he was successful in raising the INA. But it is true that he wasn't a trained soldier and, as such, it is not known whether he actively wielded arms in any battle.

If Bose were a trained and battle-tested soldier, he sure would have been with his INA fighters when they surrendered to allied forces after losing on the Imphal front.

Bose: A Radical Politician

Well before his early 1941 escape from house arrest, Bose had come to be known as a radical politician; his uneasy relationship with Mahatma Gandhi and the INC had become well known by this time. While his Indian mind had difficulty to fathom Mahatma's non-violence and non-cooperation stance, British and other Westerners took no time in understanding the challenge that Bose's radical politics threw at them. Indian public, even those who didn't agree with Gandhi's placid approach, was silently scared of the revolutionary leader's radicalism and authoritarian approach. That possibly was the reason that his ***'Forward Bloc'*** didn't make much headway with the Indian public, especially beyond Bengal. While no turbulent support emerged for Subhash's radical politics, even ardent Congressmen appreciated his integrity and commitment for freedom of the Motherland.

Western historians and commentators largely ignored Bose, or were skeptical in doing justice for his patriotic strivings. Citing misadventures of INA (as they viewed it), they attempted to prove that Bose's armed struggle piggy-riding the Japanese made little impact on the Indian freedom struggle as a whole. Some of them portrayed Bose and his soldiers as armed clowns, wholly devoid of skills and finesse of modern warfare.

On the other hand, Indians' fondness and appreciation of Bose's nationalism and struggle always stood high. Writers and political commentators never tired of sharpening the iconic image of the mysterious revolutionary that Bose had come to be viewed by the huge majority of Indian masses. And the trend continued well into the 21st century.

Bose: A Baseless Insinuation

Subhash Bose's admirers, more actively the current Hindutva elements, proffered that Jawaharlal Nehru didn't want the great patriot and freedom fighter to return to India as, in that event, the former would have instantaneously lost power—that the Indian electorate would have voted Nehru out in favour of Bose. Such an eventuality was possible but the myth is just a dreamy formation on account of the biased thoughts of such elements.

The question of Nehru wanting or not wanting Bose's post–independence return to India didn't arise as the revolutionary had died in a plane crash on August 18, 1945. Yet assuming, for a moment, that the air crash was a fabrication staged to confuse the great India revolutionary's international enemies—particularly the allied powers—in that event, the said strategy must have had the great leader's consent. It must have been part of his grand plan. Nehru had nothing to do with it.

Besides, the whole life of Subhash Bose had evidenced that he was not a weakling; he couldn't be pushed over—he always did whatsoever he wanted to do. If he were alive in the post-independence period, he could have easily sneaked into India. He was a master of disguise; he knew that he had a lot of contacts and fans ready to welcome and assist him under all circumstances.

On arrival in India, he would have surely received a great hero's welcome—and nothing could have prevented him from either activating his ***'Forward Bloc'*** or joining any political party (NDA and BJP didn't exist at that time). And the question of Nehru wanting and/or not wanting his entry into the newly-minted democracy of India didn't arise.

Subhash Bose wasn't a leader of pliant nature; he wouldn't have stayed back or gone into hiding simply because Nehru didn't want his presence in India. He wasn't ever so obedient!

What held him back, if he were alive in the post 1945 period, can never be ascertained; it is just a matter of gossip mongering or politically scented insinuations.

Jai Hind

CHAPTER 6

GANDHI-NEHRU AND BOSE

The triad of Gandhi-Nehru and Bose represented the prime force that steered the ship of Congress during 1920s and 30s. Young Subhash, after passing ICS, returned to India in 1921 and straightway went to meet Gandhi. Such was the admiration that the young Bose had for the Congress leader. Looking deeply, Gandhi and Bose were like two ends of a political pole—their philosophies and energies of thought and action differed widely—and consequently, the strategies and methods that they wanted to employ for freeing India from the long British occupation, too, weren't in full conformity. While their target objective of India's freedom was common, everything else—the means and methodologies attempted were entirely different. It is surprising that the two great leaders, in fact, worked together in the second and third decade of the 20th century—for almost seventeen years.

Bose as Congress President and Genesis of Differences

On account of his energies of thought and action, young Bose had a mercurial rise in the Indian National Congress. By 1927, he became President of the Youth Congress and his actions and statements came under watch of the British intelligence gathering agencies, which kept a tab on activities of key freedom fighters—particularly those identified as revolutionaries. He was elected as Congress President in 1938, and formed a planning committee (sort of a planning commission) which recommended speedy industrial development after the British were pushed out of India.

Bose's thoughts in regard to industrialization on lines of developments in Soviet Union sowed the first seed of differences with Gandhi. Bose, like Nehru and many other intellectuals of the era, was influenced by the rising success of industrialization in Soviet Union through its much-talked about ***'five-year plans'***. He argued in favour of making India strong through industrial development, which went against the Gandhian thoughts of village-based economy of self-sufficiency.

On this difference of thought, Nehru sided with Bose—which at that time had only a theoretical significance—and after independence, Nehru government actually followed the same script of Soviet-styled industrial development, securing technological and financial help of the rising communist regime. In addition to the above, the following areas, too, contributed to the Gandhi-Bose differences basket.

The first crack in the relationship between Gandhi and Bose emerged in 1927, when main Congress leaders were in conference with the Simon Commission, and were discussing a dominion status for India and Bose shouted:

> *"Bharat shall be free, the only question is when."*

His out of the way shouting signified indiscipline and impatience on part of the young nationalist. It went against the basic principles of the Gandhian philosophy. For a large organization that Congress had come to be recognized—with its pan-Indian presence and respect for its peaceful and disciplined methodology—this act of Bose was difficult to be condoned.

A section of the Congress identified with the strong response of Bose, while the dominant faction preferred to work with the existing Raj government from the inside. It had provoked a rare public display of anger from the Mahatma, who was the undisputed leader of the great political party.

Additionally, the following developments impacted the situation:

- In 1930s, Bose had spent several years interacting with the fascist forces in Italy and Germany, and unsuccessfully canvassed for military assistance for pushing the British out of India. It went strikingly opposite to Gandhi's approach of peaceful non-violence.
- In 1939, at Tripuri conference of Congress, Bose strongly demanded giving six months' deadline to the British to pack up and leave India. Gandhi was against such an ultimatum because attempts to implement the same were bound to turn violent. He felt that Congress had no control on numerous people who, in such a situation, were likely to turn violent. He felt that even in Congress, many people didn't listen to its management; and that furthering such an impression was injurious to its effectiveness.
- Although Gandhi appreciated political energies of Bose, the latter's active alliance in 1940s with the Axis powers—first with Nazis in Germany and then with the Nipponese regime in East Asia—weren't to Gandhi's taste. In his opinion, fascist Japanese—had they occupied India or even part of it—would have turned into more terrible imperialists than the British.
- On account of apprehensions about consequences of Bose's radical approach, Gandhi had turned against his second term as Congress president. He was elected a second time despite Gandhi's opposition, but soon resigned due to internal differences in the organization. He had made his own position in the organization unsustainable. And a crisis situation in the organization that was spearheading the campaign against the Raj, wasn't good for the country.
- There were serious differences with regard to composition of the Congress Working Committee. Bose didn't seem to work through consensus.
- In Congress, Nehru and Bose together were part of its leftist faction, and had collaborated on various issues. In 1931, both had demonstrated against the Japanese invasion of Manchuria—and then in 1938, they were critical of its invasion of China.

Gandhi's Great Appreciation for Bose

Despite the differences of ways and means as well as the strategy about fighting the British occupation of India, in 1942, Gandhi had called Bose a 'Prince among Patriots'.

And Bose, too, never lagged behind in appreciating Mahatma Gandhi. In a 1944 radio broadcast from Rangoon, he had called Gandhi the 'Father of Our Nation'.

It was the first occasion in the history of Gandhi's long struggle that someone had addressed him with such great respect. Bose did set the trend, and afterwards, it became routine for everyone to address Gandhi in this manner.

And after the August 1945 air crash demise of Bose, Gandhi was reported to have refused to believe (as per account of a nephew of Bose) that the great hero had died in the said accident. When a member of the Bose clan went with Col. Habibur Rahman, who was with the great leader in the plane but had survived the crash, to meet Gandhi in the Bhangi colony in New Delhi, the Mahatma was reported to have advised the Bose family not to perform the *shradh* ceremony for Subhash. In his opinion, Habibur Rahman was just conveying his boss's message, implying that Bose hadn't died in the crash.

But another account, possibly a more reliable one[3], stated that on hearing about the plane crash event, Gandhi had conveyed his condolences (through a telegram) to Bose's mother and other family members.

Bose was never short of controversies in his action-filled life, as well as in the mystery of his death/or disappearance. His dynamism and radical patriotism—and his selection of ways and means often fuelled controversies.

Bose's Mercurial Rise in Congress

After joining the Congress, rise of Bose to the top was phenomenal. On Gandhi's advice, he went to Calcutta under the mentorship of CR Das and became a very prominent figure in the city. His political rise was alarming to such an extent that the British Criminal Investigation

Department started keeping tabs on him (he was the youngest politician to have this "honour").

He was selected to be the president of the Youth Congress, was imprisoned, was released, and by 1927, he was one of the general secretaries of Congress. It was during these years that the 'relationship between Jawaharlal Nehru and Bose' was cemented as well. This aspect of the relationship between Gandhi, Nehru and Bose was important, which many Indian intellectuals fail to appreciate in right measure. They attempt to see more conflict in the relationship than there actually was.

In fact, all good relationships do have some content of disagreement; otherwise the same would dry up for want of dialogue or energy interaction.

Nehru was attributed with the following remark about the Indian Civil Service:

> *"Indian Civil Service, with which we are unfortunately still afflicted in this country, is neither Indian and civil, nor a service."*

This remark possibly contributed to the factors which made Bose quit the ICS and join Gandhi and Congress in the first place.

Why did Nehru make the remark stated above? His sole intention, possibly, was to dissuade Bose from getting tied up with a service that the freedom fighters didn't see bearing any positivity. Nehru had seen an action-filled politician and patriot in Subhash Bose, and he didn't want him to get wasted with the said service.

Bose was inspired by Bal Gangadhar Tilak (radical) and Gandhiji was into the tradition of Gopal Krishna Gokhale (moderate), and their approach towards India's struggle for independence reflected the basic attitude difference too.

Nehru-Bose Camaraderie

Nehru and Bose worked closely during major part of the latter's time with the Congress. They were both socialists, whereas Rajagopalachari (or Rajaji), Rajendra Prasad and Sardar Patel formed a right-wing association (informal in nature) in the Congress. Between Bose and Nehru, Congress remained a political body with a socialistic agenda as they held (or someone close to them held) the post of Congress president. The right wing of the Congress had no chance against the combined influence of Nehru and Bose on the cadres of the great party.

It was in 1927 that Bose pressed for the ***"Purna Swaraj"*** resolution, but it was easily defeated by others in 1928. However, it was adopted in a different form in 1942.

The Dandi Salt March of 1930 was actively praised by Bose, about which he drew parallels and compared it with Napoleon's march on Paris. He said that just like the march of Napoleon, Gandhi's march would change the course of history: which is exactly what happened.

Interestingly, Nehru was vocally apprehensive about this move. In the First Round Table Conference chaired by King George, the Congress was not invited. However, in the Second Round Table Conference, Gandhi was invited as the sole representative of Congress. He attended the conference with Sarojini Naidu, and it turned into a battle for minority rights because of tactical British support to Dr B R Ambedkar. As a consequence, the larger goal of freedom suffered a setback.

Bose was disappointed, to say the least, on two fronts: Gandhi's stand on minority issues, and his failure to speak boldly for freedom of the country.

After this incident, Bose visited many European countries as he was suffering with depression. He had met Mussolini in Italy, got married in Germany—and was influenced by Garibaldi, who was famous for his following quote:

> *"I offer neither pay and quarters, nor food; I offer only hunger, thirst, forced marches, battles and death. Let him, who loves his country with his heart and not merely with his lips, follow me."*

This, coupled with the story of the victory of Garibaldi against the French, had a tremendous influence on Bose.

When Bose returned to India in 1938, he still had deep respect for Gandhi, but criticized his ways—chief among them being modernization, which was much more prevalent in Europe and its impact was visible to one and all.

Gandhi with his *'charkha'* (the spinning wheel) seemed too old-fashioned for Bose to reconcile with, on long-term basis.

Wounded Bengali Psyche

Bengali intelligentsia, including most of the members of the large Bose clan, hasn't cured itself of the victim syndrome that it acquired instantaneously on death/or disappearance of Subhash Bose. The damage to the psyche of a section of the community continues even after the lapse of over seven decades. It might last many more decades, because there is no logical attempt to minimize or eliminate the same.

The paranoia seems to have gone so deep that, overtly and/or covertly, they blame Nehru for their loss. They forget that:

(a) It wasn't Nehru who threw Subhash into the deadly embrace of fascist Japanese (and earlier the European ones);

(b) And that the latter was on the aerial escapade out of his own will and plan when the air crash occurred, or the act of disappearance was enacted.

Nehru had no role whatsoever in the said event. Madhuri Bose's recent work, *The Bose Brothers and Indian Independence: An Insider's Account*, as per a commentator in the New Year Special issue of Tehelka (vi), was reported to have expressed the family's anguish on the eve of freedom, as under:

> *"Sarat (elder of the Bose brothers) sat quietly on the first floor southern verandah of his Woodburn park home in Calcutta. He had fought like a Lion to prevent the partition with all its tragic consequences; the India of his and Subhas' dreams had not materialized, and Bengal was cleaved down the middle. And India as a dominion within the British empire, accepted by Nehru still had to achieve the complete independence on which the brothers had never compromised. The British Raj both admired and feared the Bose brothers."*

The assigning of blame on to Nehru is clear; forgetting that it wasn't Nehru alone who had accepted the division of India. Gandhi, Jinnah and a significant number of senior leaders were involved. The Bose family's grudge, however, centered on and around Nehru because he had become the Prime Minister, while the fate of Subhash Bose was clouded in uncertainties.

The damage to the Bengali psyche was so intense that despite passage of over seven decades and Bose family having enjoyed several positions of importance at center and in the state, it continued to bleed. Unable to reconcile to the irreparable loss in form of Subhash's death/ or disappearance, several theories and myths were promoted. Over the years, no one has tried to clear up the question shrouded in mystery: ***"What prevented Bose (if he had escaped the air crash alive) from walking into his dear independent India and reclaiming his distinguished position?"***

The so-called split between Bose and Nehru is always highlighted, while their collaborations and consistent leftist tendencies always ignored. That any two leaders are never fully co-centric for their ideas and policies—they must differ for a healthy democracy, is never given deserved consideration.

That Subhash had resigned from Congress president-ship on account of his inability to deal with seniors and colleagues is conveniently forgotten. Nehru's pleadings in favour of INA soldiers at the Red Fort, too, are often twisted out of context. The wounded psyche never stopped working at its active pace.

Jai Hind

CHAPTER 7

GUMNAMI BABA AND SUBHASH BOSE

On and off, for over three decades, the story of Gumnami Baba of Faizabad has been making rounds in the Indian media. It is suspected that the same was fuelled purposefully by some fans of Netaji and some individuals and agencies that still see residual value in keeping the myth of the great leader's death /or disappearance. Possibly, some Bose family members, too, played a role in appearance of such reports. For these people, the legend of Subhash Bose must become ***'chiranjivi'***, much like that of the mythological Hanuman. The latest of the Gumnami Baba episodes appeared in the national press (post-declassification of the Bose files by the GOI and the TMC government in West Bengal) on March 16, 2016 in the Times of India. The report was titled (vii):

> *"Netaji family photos found in Gumnami Baba's trove."*
> *"Letters by INA veterans recovered."*

It was a non-investigated report designed to keep the Netaji's death/ or disappearance myth evergreen, incentive being the upcoming elections in West Bengal. For sure, local press must have picked it up for whatsoever value it was worth for the gullible public. Interesting parts of the said press report are reproduced below:

"The mystery surrounding Gumnami Baba, who many believe was Subhash Chandra Bose living incognito in UP's Faizabad, turned deeper on Tuesday (15th March, 2016) with the recovery of old photographs of the Bose family from the district's treasury."

"Apart from family portrait, there is a photograph of Netaji's parents Jaankinath and Prabhadevi Bose in the inventory—their identities confirmed by Shakti Singh, the owner of the Ram Bhawan, where Gumnami Baba spent the final years of his life from1982 to 1985."

"The family photograph of the Bose family shows 22 members besides his parents, said Singh, who is also a special invitee to the committee formed by the Faizabad administration for the retrieval and cross-verification of Gumnami Baba's artifacts."

"Singh said Lalita Bose, the daughter of Netaji's brother Suresh, had visited Ram Bhawan in Faizabad on February 4, 1986. She identified the people in the photographs when these were at Ram Bhawan and the description Lalita provided is part of the inventory."

"Apart from this, a number of telegrams sent to Gumnami Baba by Azad Hind Fauz veterans Pabitra Mohan Roy (senior officer of INA's intelligence wing) and Sunil Kant Gupta on the occasions of Durga Puja and 23 January (Netaji's birthday) have also been found."

"Gumnami Baba had a habit of making indirect references of people. He referred to Sunil Kant Gupta as Sukriti. Some letters mentioning the names of sender's as Mukul and Tripti were also found, Singh told the TOI."

"Singh heads the S C Bose Rastriya Vichar Kendra in Faizabad. He said the documents retrieved from Ram Bhawan indicate that the Baba was not just another sage, but an extraordinary human being."

As per the author, the report had multilateral gaps or deficiencies, some of which were:

Did members of Bose family visit the Ram Bhawan when Baba was alive?

Were they not aware of his presence?

The INA veterans who wrote letters and sent telegrams to Baba—why didn't they inform any member of the large Bose family in this regard?

Singh, the owner of the Ram Bhawan, hasn't clarified whether 'Baba' came with the entire luggage or where from he had come to this place.

And what was so special about Faizabad that attracted the Baba (apparently Subhash Bose) to this place?

Surely, any house owner must know at least some basic facts about his or her long-staying guest.

Justice Mukherjee Commission, amongst others, investigated the matter related to the Gumnami Baba and in absence of any convincing evidence (by owner of the Ram Bhawan, Bose family members and the Faizabad administration), rubbished the theory that the said Baba was Subhash Bose.

Some associates of Subhash Bose had formed a "Subhasbadi Janta" primarily to promote a story that Bose was the chief hermit of an ashram at Saulmari in North Bengal. They engaged themselves with spreading rumours and illusions about Subhash Bose, and benefited from the sale of published materials on this hugely emotional issue.

Never, in the long decades after the great hero's death/ or disappearance, have his fans, friends and family members clarified why Bose had to become a hermit; why he had not come out openly and contributed to the building of our nation. Is it possible that a passionate man like Subhash Bose, who had such a large family, fan-following and ex-colleagues in India as well as abroad, shall keep wholly silent for such a long time?

Often, Bose family members, fans as well as some MPs and MLAs (in West Bengal), over a period of time, have claimed that Soviet Union was blackmailing Nehru—and later even Indira Gandhi—for not disclosing the whereabouts of Subhash Bose. None of them, however, ever explained why several BJP and NDA governments that ruled Delhi, off and on during the past over four decades, didn't disclose the matter for everyone's benefit.

Was their anti-Congress posture only a part of an attention seeking plan?

RSS's Attempts to muddy the Bose Mystery

The March 16, 2016 issue of the Times of India also carried an RSS-Netaji related story titled as (viii):

> *"RSS ex-chief's letter junks crash theory."*

The story went as under:

> *"A letter written by the RSS fifth chief, K S Sudershan, on June 7, 2007 categorically states Netaji Subhash Chandra Bose returned from Russia in or around 1953, and lived as Gumnami Baba in different parts of the country."*

"The letter was found on Tuesday, days after one by RSS' second Sarsanghchalak M S Golwalkar, was found among Gumnami Baba's effects in the Faizabad treasury. Sudershan's letter addressed to Shakti Singh, the owner of the Ram Bhawan, where the Gumnami Baba lived the final years of his life, states that the news of Netaji's death in Taihoku plane crash was 'presumed' to be true. But the truth is that two of India's ambassadors to Russia—Vijaya Laxshmi Pandit and S Radhakrishnan—had met Netaji in person inside the jail. Sudershan writes, adding that both the ambassadors were instructed not to spread the news about Bose's survival. It is for this neglect (meted out to Netaji) that he was forced to lead life as Gumnami Baba, either in the Himalayas or in and around Ayodhya. Sudershan further added that for long, people of the country had no knowledge about him."

"The same letter was also published in my book *Bhagwanji se Netaji Tak* in December 2008," said Singh, adding that Sudarshan at times regretted that RSS could not act in time to help Bose."

"On April 23, 2006, speaking in Kolkata, Sudarshan had claimed Netaji was alive till 1985 and did not die in the Taihoku air crash. Sudershan had also demanded that the Justice M K Mukherjee Commission on Netaji be sent to Russia by the then UPA government to examine the relevant documents."

The Sudarshan story, too, is an example of poor journalism; it has, among others, the following holes visible even to a casual reader:

Why didn't Sudarshan pursue with the NDA government and get to the bottom of the matter? Why did it occur to him after the NDA was replaced by the UPA?

Sudarshan, despite being the RSS chief, didn't obviously understand the basic nature of Bose's personality. He was not someone who could be made to do things which weren't wholly to his liking. Right after arrival in India (if he ever arrived), could he be forced to become a hermit against his will? Was he not a man of strong determination? To presume so will be a great insult to the persona of our great revolutionary.

What was RSS' compulsion that prevented it from helping Bose at the right time, i.e. when he was alive and roamed as a hermit?

Why is Shakti Singh waking up now? Was he not part of the conspiracy (if any) to keep a cover on Netaji's presence as a hermit?

With whose help was Netaji released from Russian jail, if he came to India in 1953?

Why the NDA government didn't clarify the issue related to the two Indian ambassadors having met Bose in Russian jail? What stopped them from declassifying the information if the same existed in government files? Didn't Sudershan have enough clout to get this simple job done?

The fact that RSS and NDA have been actively muddying the Bose mystery solely for political purposes can't be hidden from discerning public eyes. These efforts had a dubious purpose—on one hand, it was aimed at sullying Congress' image through misuse of an emotion-intense issue, and to gather sympathy of Bose's fans and admirers on the other. On both fronts, its success has been almost insignificant.

Jai Hind

CHAPTER 8

QUESTIONS NEEDING CLARIFICATION

While studying the life and works of Subhash Bose which were aimed at freeing India from the imperialistic control of British, one encounters numerous unanswered and/or unanswerable questions. Several situations of his engagements (i.e. the acts of omission and commission) in the massive job aren't fully understood or adequately researched. Some of these are highlighted below:

Ways and Means Conflict

The first and foremost of these situations is based upon the well-documented truth that Bose had basic differences with Gandhiji and other senior leaders of Congress with regards to ***'ways and means'*** adopted in furthering the freedom struggle. In contrast to Gandhi's non-violent methods—namely Satyagraha and peaceful agitations—Bose advocated a violent struggle for throwing the British out of India.

Did he understand the extent of bloodshed that a violent struggle in such a large country, divided by numerous religions and languages, was bound to create? Were the resources and organization needed for managing such a rebellion or covert combat—and eventual civil war—understood and appreciated in requisite depth?

The obvious answer for both the vital questions is a capital no. In those years, Bose hadn't seen and/or experienced horrors of a war. Horrors of the WW I hadn't directly affected India—and by the time the great war concluded, Bose was just in the process of stepping into adulthood. He had no idea of the scale of loss of life and properties if a widespread civil war was to take place. We don't know to what extent and in what depth he had studied the 1857 mutiny or the first war of India's independence. Had he done that, the young revolutionary would have neither advocated employment of violent means against the British occupiers, nor would his ways and means approach have had greater similarity to that of his Italian hero, Giuseppe Garibaldi.

And there is no evidence to suggest that enough planning was done for directing/controlling a widespread violent struggle, or if the resources needed for the same were worked upon. Nowhere does one find the evidence of an action plan with all the needed components for the purpose of launching and sustaining a local violent rebellion that could have lasted for many years. British wouldn't have given up control on a golden bird that India was once known, in any easy manner.

There is a lot of difference between talking of a violent struggle in a conference room or in a meeting, and in factually arranging one to emerge and grow to yield planned results.

Why No Guerrilla Action?

Why the leftist group, called the ***'Forward Bloc'*** that Bose created, wasn't turned into a militant guerrilla organization? Why resources for the same weren't collected? Why, like Mao Zedong, he didn't put emphasis on revolt initiating and spreading from India's villages, making it a people's struggle? Why did he concentrate on issuing statements and making speeches only in urban areas where nothing could escape attention of British intelligence agents? Was he a conference room or radio talk show revolutionary? No researcher or commentator seems to have answered these and related questions with any justification.

Why didn't he appreciate the massive strength of people that he could gather in the country? Why did the struggle of 1857 not give him some foresight as how to go about a violent struggle? His appeal among the Indian youth wasn't only substantial but almost unlimited—then why did he not take advantage of it?

India had a large number of *rajas*, *maharajas* and *nawabs* with immense resources in terms of people, finance and weaponry. It is not clear from available literature why this great source of inputs for tagging a home-grown violent struggle wasn't explored? Instead, Subhash Bose, our great revolutionary, put faith in fascist powers of that time. He must have had his logic for looking outwards—but the same is not understood properly; his fans and admirers seem almost totally ignorant in this regard.

This question, to some extent, can possibly be explained in light of the Bengali psyche of arguing in detail on any issue but often falling short of initiating some concrete planned action. Bose was primarily a ***'dialogist'***—initiator of an argument and winner of the same. He wasn't an implementer. During his Congress days, he did his best to excite the organization and its component members to shun non-violence, and start a violent struggle. But Gandhi's strong influence negated the same. In fact, members of the then Congress weren't trained for conducting an armed struggle—and even if one was initiated somehow, they wouldn't have carried it forward. On the other side of the Himalayas, Mao Zedong had understood the requirements of such a struggle in necessary depth—and that is why he worked through villagers who could take strains of combat that are inherent in an armed struggle.

Why did Bose always prefer to take help from the outside? The philosophy behind this approach has never been clarified by any of his co-workers and/or associates. Historians— Indian as well as foreign—ignored this critical issue, too. No one, in fact, seems to have been able to decode Bose's logic in this regard.

Most of the revolutionaries of the past two centuries, who fought tyrant regimes and eventually freed their people employing violent means, depended primarily upon local resources. From outside, one can organize invasions, but revolutions normally need to sprout and grow in local soil. Hundreds of invasions of India were effected from outside, primarily from across the Hindukush, while not even a single revolution travelled to India from the other side of its borders.

Answers to all of the above questions seem to probably reside in the fact that Bose came from urban upper class; his exposure to rural India was limited. His rebellions started from college class rooms and travelled to conference and meeting rooms. It is difficult to believe that he didn't know how to take his rebellious ideas to rural youth who could bear rigours of guerrilla fighting force or a hit, run and hide organization.

The second part of the reason possibly was that he wasn't a trained military-man. He possibly didn't know how to organize groups of fighters who could attack British establishments and then melt into the vastness of rural and/or urban India.

Thirdly, the European fascists and their anti-British positions fascinated Bose. He thought, rightly or wrongly, that the job of pushing the British occupiers out of India could be delegated to the anti-British powers, or that they could be excited to enable non-resident Indians do the job. That formulation sadly formed the foundation for Bose's eventual failure.

Further, his '**Forward Bloc**' adherents mainly comprised the ***'verbal warriors'*** who didn't know, or weren't trained for wielding firearms, kill and be killed. Bengali rebels of 1st and 2nd decades of the 20th century never graduated beyond making crude bombs and sometimes throwing the same. There were no Maoists at that time from whom Subhash and his followers could learn how to use violent means to their advantage. But instances of the freedom struggle of 1857 weren't too old, or impossible to duplicate. And there were numerous international instances which could have served as learning and practicing tools for waging an armed struggle.

Fighting Independent of Japanese

Subhash had done a marvelous job of turning the INA—initially a ragtag assemblage of British Indian soldiers who had surrendered to Japanese in the East Asia, plus some local volunteers—into an excellent fighting outfit. There were limitations of having a super-boss in form of the Japanese military machine, yet the achievements of INA were indeed great.

However, all through the early half of 1945, strong trends were emerging on war fronts suggesting that eventually the Axis forces were going to lose the war. Then, why did Bose and his commanders not work upon the possibilities of fighting independently, if and when the Japanese surrendered? Why was there no plan B for difficult situations?

Explanation to the above rests, perhaps, in the fact that a standalone approach for fighting the Raj forces was never thought about. Additionally, Bose's views on invincibility of the Axis powers had possibly clouded his and his commanders' thinking—or his commanders didn't like to suggest a line of action that went contrary to their leader's thinking.

When things turned tough or started going wrong, why didn't the key formations of INA decide to turn into guerilla units and melt into the vastness of forests and mountains of the Indo-Burma terrains to fight and harass British forces in an effective manner? There is no evidence to confirm that skills for persevering, independent of the Japanese, were developed in the INA outfits. The forests of Naga Hills and Arakan range were deep enough to provide the needed cover. After independence, several Naga and other tribal rebel groups flourished in the same hills and forests. Weren't food and arms easily available to them? These rebel formations continued to trouble Indian security forces well into the 21st century.

Surrendering with INA Soldiers

Another, and probably the most important, question remains—why did Netaji not surrender along with his combatants and commanders of the INA? British Raj administration surely wouldn't have hung him; none of the surrendered INA soldiers and officers was punished. Bose knew well that WW II had weakened the British imperialists beyond repair or recovery. Then why did this non-professional decision occur on part of the great hero? Or was he under pressure from the Japanese to not fall into British hands? This question, too, has never been investigated or discussed in needed detail either by his critics and/or his fans.

When the Japanese themselves were going through a dishonourable surrender, of what use was Bose to them? Why did they want him, or help him, escape to Manchuria? Was it an expression of their loyalty to each other? Nothing on the matter, or on other related issues, has ever been said or clarified by any of Bose's numerous biographers and critics.

What happened to INA Treasures?

It is said that during his aerial escape, Bose carried several steel trunks or packages containing the treasures (the INA war chest). What happened to these valuables? It is even more important to know as to why the great warrior didn't distribute these valuables amongst his suffering soldiers and/or commandants of the INA? These were funds of a collective ownership. Did Bose want to use these valuables and cash to raise another fighting force, possibly with Russian help?

In fact, Stalin—right in 1941—had snubbed Bose, and the latter had to fall back upon the Nazis; so how come Bose was optimistic of Russian help in an adverse situation like that of August 1945?

Why Is There No Official Record of Plane Crash?

Why was there no official record of the 18th August 1945 plane crash in Taiwan, which then was under Japanese control? Was the chaos of Japanese defeat and resultant surrender responsible for it—or the Japanese authorities didn't want to create evidence of Bose's death? What could be the real motive behind the same has never been clarified. Several eye witnesses—including the doctor and nurse who attended to the wounded Bose along with that of the great hero's own ADC (Col. Habibur Rahman) while deposing before several investigating committees and commissions—confirmed the cruel accident. Why the same were discarded by those who wanted to believe that our great hero wasn't dead but lived to eventually free us from the British slavery, or later on come to free India from debilitating chains of inefficiency, corruption and mal-administration?

Difference of Opinion in the Bose Family

Why didn't the illustrious Bose family have some unity of opinion and/ or assessment with regard to the great hero's death/or disappearance? Why did they differ so widely? Were some of the Bose brothers, nephews and nieces motivated by their own individual objectivities? Or was it a normal expression of a large family's diverse interests? This bothers fans and admirers of the great freedom fighter a great deal.

Differences of opinion within the large Bose family have been starkly visible with regard to the death and/or disappearance myth. Bose's daughter Anita, who lived in Germany, strongly believed that her father died in the 18th August 1945 plane crash tragedy. Several members of the mainstream of the large family not only believed otherwise, but expressed annoyance on the Indo-German girl's difference of opinion.

Files Declassification Drama

Why has the mystery of Bose's death/or disappearance not been solved despite declassification of files by the GOI and also the Trinamool Congress government of West Bengal? Is the mystery wholly unsolvable? Or are there some records beyond reach of one and all?

It is perhaps too late to solve the death/ or disappearance mystery of Subhash Bose based upon the files lying in GOI's custody. May be the files with the British, Russians and Japanese governments can help!

And it is more than sure that information that might emerge in future, irrespective of source, is bound to create only newer controversies, or strengthen the old ones. Total clarity is unlikely in this vastly complex matter.

RSS and Subhash Bose

RSS was never sympathetic to Subhash Bose's mission of winning freedom from the British through employment of violent means or military assistance from outside forces. Numerous Janta Dal, BJP-supported and/or NDA governments which, off and on, ruled India for several years during the past three decades, didn't solve the mystery of

Bose death and /or disappearance. Why suddenly, in the 2nd decade of the 21st century, RSS and NDA turned keen on the issue? No one from the Saffron brigade or the NDA family seems to attend to this crucial question.

There are several other questions raised at different places of this work. They need to be answered—and today, for the purpose, NDA is the best equipped outfit for the said purpose. Now, they must do the job with full sincerity. No excuses can be tolerated since they don't have the alleged narrow interests of Congress, or the Nehru-Gandhi outfit. And the large Bose family is whole-heartedly with them.

Let the Modi government gather or grab all the relevant files from Moscow, London and Tokyo, and make them public. It would be the true service to the memory of the great revolutionary of India.

Jai Hind

CHAPTER 9

SOME GREAT MISTAKES MADE BY BOSE

Everyone who takes decisions, in business or in military operations, is entitled to make some mistakes—big or small—because they can't be fully avoided. All actions have the possibility of turning unpalatable with the passage of time, or when analyzed in changed situations. It is not wholly bad to make mistakes. However, it is bad to repeat the same and suffer unacceptable losses or damages.

Big or small, all people tend to make mistakes. Wiser ones do mid-course corrections while others persist with what has been done and even attempt to justify the same. Hitler had erred when during WW II he decided to attack Russia, with which the process of German defeat commenced. Similarly, Nipponese had committed the blunder, in utter over-estimation of their capabilities, of attacking the Pearl Harbor located at the Pacific coast of USA. It drew Americans into the war, and it was the US participation in the war on side of anti-fascist forces that finally turned the tide of the WW II.

Much earlier, Napoleon had made the grave mistake of going full blast against Russia and, as a consequence, lost credibility as a great general. More recently, Soviet Union had committed the mistake of intervening in Afghanistan. Americans despite being democrats erred a great deal, first by going to Vietnam and then barging into Afghanistan and Iraq. They helped in spawning and spreading of terrorism the world over.

Back home, even under a democratic setup, Jawaharlal Nehru, Indira Gandhi and almost all other politicians who followed, made mistakes that left varied adverse impact on the nation's internal and international fabric.

Bose had worked under stressful environments and taken up a goal that was indeed most challenging. And he elected to select '***ways and means***' for achieving his objective, with which many people didn't agree. He annoyed many people; and his adversaries in form of the British imperialists, assisted by the Americans, were indeed awesome. They were a great empire. And in a situation of confronting it, Bose was not only destined to face great problems—some mistakes were bound to occur in the process, through acts of omission and commission.

Not Turning into a Covert Fighter

Covert operations, or guerrilla warfare, are normally the low input and efficient way of fighting established rulers and/or exploitative regimes. History is full of such examples, where bands of committed mobile and covert fighters have over-thrown large, corrupt and insensitive rulers/dictators. Fidel Castro and Mao Zedong are the two not too old examples. And over a century ago, Garibaldi had done an excellent job with a small force of covert and mobile co-combatants as well.

In case of Subhash Bose, not turning his ***'Forward Bloc'*** into a covert militant organization was possibly the first great mistake on part of the great revolutionary. In his own den, with massive support of local revolutionaries and his outstanding skills of disguise and escape, Bose sure could have easily turned into a Castro or Mao of India in a short time because Gandhi's non-violent struggle and then WW II had weakened the imperialists a lot. In four to five years of intense covert indigenous operations, Bose surely would have pushed the British occupiers out of India one or two years before 1947. And the great revolutionary would have had a chance to rule India for a long time. But fate had turned against him.

For organizing an effective violent thrust for throwing the British out of India, there was no dearth of committed local young men ready for enlistment as covert fighters. There was no dearth of sentiments in his favour. And there existed a lot of hills and forests to provide cover to enact hit-and-run operations.

Local finance for support to such a cadre and weapons, too, wouldn't have been a problem. Nationalist businessmen would sure have contributed willingly. There was sympathy in mind of the population towards all types of freedom fighters. Indian police and military units, too, had sympathetic elements. Stories of 1857 revolt or mutiny were still fresh. Why did Bose not attempt organizing insurgency? He was good at disguising after all. This puzzle has never been analyzed.

Afterwards, militants in the Northeast India did an excellent job of covert operations, and since mid-1960s, local Maoist in the Red Corridor demonstrated feasibility of covert war so efficiently. British occupiers didn't have the time that governments in democratic India have, and they sure would have run out of India without much fuss.

Association with Fascists

Before Bose decided to escape to Europe, he sure must have debated the local militant option. Possibly, he couldn't gather enough confidence amongst his local friends, fans and supporters for the massive job, or he feared the ruthlessness of British governance. May be not being a trained military man came in his way, or his family members dissuaded him from a local option.

Once in Europe, he didn't have much of option; by force of circumstances, he had to go to the German fascists. Russians had shown lack of interest and Italians were occupied with their neighborhood struggles. Through high grade diplomacy, good selling skills and perseverance, Bose was to generate enough interest among the Germans to come forward and offer some help.

Bose succeeded more with the Japanese fascists then with the Germans. In the short-term, his INA did a good job at the Indo Burma border and in Naga Hills. But destiny hadn't planned for him to walk victoriously into Delhi and rule the country.

Bose had selected the option of working with the fascists for attempting liberation of India employing military force. With that decision, it wasn't possible for him to fully avoid getting some adverse image colouration.

Not Prompting INA to go underground

INA earned glory in its battles at the Indo-Burma border. Circumstances defeated this newly minted nationalistic force. An over 40,000-soldiers' army didn't collapse in a day; it took time. The circumstances of its defeat are well known; what is not known is why a core group of fighters, just a few hundred of them, didn't elect to go underground in hills and forests on the Indo-Burma border. As a covert force attacking British at a place and time of its choice could have easily afforded it a few years' time as a guerilla unit harassing the imperialists on one hand, and avoiding the tag of total surrender on the other. And as the British colonists had weakened a lot on account of the effect of the Great War, independence of India was just a year or so away.

Why was such a decision not taken despite the fact that INA had some guerilla units and had good committed commanders? Bose was probably not attuned to jungle warfare—or did he have faith only in power confrontations of large armies? Whatever the reason for not electing to go underground, Bose and his INA lost the chance of soon walking gloriously to Delhi. Only the year 1946 was in between.

Not Surrendering Along with INA Soldiers

As a good commander and leader of people, alternate to going underground with a select core of fighters, Bose should have elected to surrender with his INA soldiers and commanders. It would have been more honourable for the great fighting force. It would have done full justice to the name and fame of the first national army of independent India. In that case, reception at India's Red Fort would have been truly memorable.

British imperialists who were greatly weakened on account of numerous battles of WW II on one hand, and loss of confidence in loyalty of the British Indian Army, on the other, would have possibly decided to pack their bags even without attempting trials at the Red Fort. British sure wouldn't have had the guts to punish Bose, let alone hang him. Situation was different; their hands were weak.

And sure, we would have had a great leader to lead the independent India democratically or otherwise.

Quite possibly, with his great diplomatic skills, MA Jinnah and his Muslim League would have given up demand for Pakistan. It is a dream scenario—but the rare possibility of it coming true, or even a thought of it, is a soothing one.

Inability to Stop Japanese Torture and Cruelties in Andaman and Nicobar

Japanese had occupied the Indian territories of Andaman and Nicobar islands. After the war, the Tokyo War Crimes Tribunal had carefully documented the atrocities committed by Japanese occupiers throughout these territories, almost on daily basis.

Former Japanese officers testified that these territories remained under Japanese control all through the years of war, despite superficial goodwill shown to Bose and his commanders. Brutalities were inflicted on the Indian islanders on minor suspicion of loyalty to the Raj. Their methods were indeed cruel. Summary executions weren't uncommon. Testimonies highlighted that some Indians preferred suicides to facing Japanese atrocities. It is not that Bose wasn't aware of these atrocities, he just chose to keep quiet and didn't protest strongly enough. Possibly, his long association with fascists had dulled his sensitivities. Netaji had visited these territories but did nothing to get relief for the so-called liberated people. In chapter 10 of his book '***The Falling Tiger***', Marshall J. Getz rendered a brief description of Japanese atrocities on Indian people and Bose's failure to get the same stopped. It is a heart-rending account of what took place and more than worth a read for Indian citizens so they know what our ancestors had to go through for the independence we enjoy today.

Jai Hind

CHAPTER 10

BOSE'S PLACE AMONGST NATIONALISTS AND REVOLUTIONARIES

Indians consider Bose as the greatest Indian revolutionary of modern times. Some of them place him even above Mahatma Gandhi, with whom he had worked for several long years. The two, guru as well as the disciple, tried to modify each other's philosophy and methodology of revolutions. On account of the total irreconcilability of their methods and means, they parted ways after long years of trying—but respected each other a great deal all through their lives.

Bose has gained a permanent place in hearts and minds of people of South Asia; beyond India's borders to the East as well as to the West, people remember him with utmost respect and pride. He had his own philosophy which primarily seemed to have been based upon ideals and approaches of Lok Manya Tilak, who was the first Indian freedom fighter to have advocated use of violent means against the British imperialistic occupation of India.

Bose, having been influenced by Tilak, had selected a methodology for freeing India from the exploitative British imperialists through the use of military means—not so much through indigenous efforts but primarily by securing the same from international adversaries of the British occupiers of India. By the time Bose had landed on the revolutionary canvas of India, the 20th century had seen the world divided into two broad groups—the Western powers headed by Britain and supported by France, USA and others like Australia and Canada, and another, the fascist forces led by Italy and Germany.

Russia had gone through the strenuous pangs of the '***Great October Revolution***', and after Vladimir Lenin, another fascist dictator named Stalin was in control of the Soviet Union. Communism was on ascendance and leftists of India, including the young Bose, were greatly influenced by the same.

Tilak had made deep impression on the revolutionary psyche of young Subhash Bose. He had made great sacrifices, went to jail a number of times and for years attempted to secure foreign military support for fulfilling his stated objective. He persisted against discouragement that resulted from initial lack of interest of anti-British powers in India's struggle and Bose's scheme of things. From his position, of a left leaning activist with the Indian National Congress in 1920s and 30s, he took a turn to gel with the leading fascists of the world—and eventually turned into a famed commander of INA combatants. He developed high level of diplomatic skills, and was able to deal with highest authorities of anti-British regimes with ease of a seasoned professional.

Subhash Bose was a forceful communicator and the Axis powers loved his capabilities of propaganda against the allied powers, especially the British. He worked with second hand military resources i.e. the INA combatants, most of who earlier worked in the British Indian Army and were captured by the Axis powers. Bose's superior motivational skills raised the so composed INA into a great fighting force.

But with all said and done, he and his INA for circumstances beyond their control, failed in final moments. Its victory remained limited to India's eastern border and primarily for circumstances beyond its control, could not march triumphantly to Delhi.

Was it a case of misfortune or mismanagement? We do not know. Whatsoever the cause, Bose as a revolutionary and nationalist lost the chance of ruling the people of India that he thought about and dreamt for, on a full time basis.

For long-term impact of a nationalist and/or revolutionary upon his or her people's psyche, an analysis and evaluation of such efforts can be attempted employing the following yardsticks:

(a) motivation expertise;
(b) resources generation;
(c) military strategy;
(d) ideology employed;
(e) foreign occupation;
(f) diplomatic expertise;
(g) localization of revolution; and
(h) people's involvement in the effort.

In this comparative evaluation, two great revolutionaries of the 20th century who employed ideology coupled with violent means—Lenin and Mao Zedong—are considered. Among the nationalists who fought against dictators employing violent means, Fidel Castro and Che Guerra are picked up for their extraordinary exploits. The nationalists who fought occupiers with outside military help included Charles De-Gaul of France and Subhash Bose of India. And the peaceful revolutionaries are Mahatma Gandhi and Nelson Mandela.

Lenin and Mao

Vladimir Lenin played the most important role in creating and directing the Russian Revolution, which not only changed basic socio-cultural fabric of the country but in due course, influenced many other nations all over the globe going red. From 1950s to 1980s, Russian communism influenced a large number of countries in Europe, Asia, Africa and Latin America. His motivational expertise was par-excellence. He channelized Marx's philosophy to energize peasants and factory workers into a massive force of agitators—occupying urban centers, industries, legislatures, and forcing the autocratic rulers to abdicate and finally be executed.

Communism as an ideology of governance gained wide acceptance under his directions. He employed purely local resources in terms of workers and peasants for not only causing revolution, but for spreading and stabilizing the same. He was possibly the greatest leader of the proletariat that the world has ever known.

Stalin, who followed Lenin, consolidated what was done by his predecessor. But he soon turned into a massive dictator. He wasn't a revolutionary. He caused the world to be divided into two large camps during the Cold War years, lasting for about four decades and then fading out by early 1990s. Intense military revelry was the result and at several points, during his rule and that of his successors, the world was at edge of a nuclear war.

Lenin and his followers worked entirely with their indigenous resources—material as well as non-material. They lent support to emerging communist movements in several countries across continents. Bose, as a revolutionary, didn't fully understand the key role of local resources—human as well as material —and that possibly was the reason that despite great sacrifices, he received only partial success.

Mao Zedong

Mao was just four years senior to Subhash Bose. Contrary to Bose, he was born in a peasant family, and this was possibly the reason for difference in the two great leaders' style of nationalism and revolutionary outputs. Mao didn't go to English schools; he struggled through the rugged rural Chinese environment of early decades of the 20th century.

Han Suyin[5], in beginning of '**The Morning Deluge**', employed the following beautiful words to describe Mao:

> *"I thought then of Chairman Mao as both the child and the leader of the revolution; the nation man and also the man-ocean; the student of their people as well as their teacher; the one who represents and articulates their genius and also is most indebted to that genius; the builder of a New China; and the destroyer of that worst of all Chinese traditions: submission and obedience to the ruler."*

Can we say something similar about Subhash Bose? Partly yes and partly no! Bose was more of a nationalist; he didn't so much cause a revolution.

He didn't learn much from the Indian people, nor was he their teacher. He always looked outside for help—to pull his chestnuts out of fire. And that led to his failure as a revolutionary who made a lot of noise but failed to finish the job at hand.

Unlike Bose, Mao was a great finisher; he ensured that his projects reached conclusive ends irrespective of all odds.

What Suyin said about Mao Zedong, to a large extent, was possibly true of Mahatma Gandhi, who learnt from his people and worked through and with them. He caused and sustained the ***'revolution of peaceful non-violent struggle'*** for freedom against the British occupiers, never raising a stick or even a finger against them. He was truly a nation man and also the man-ocean.

Here, Bose came near to being a nation man too. But he wasn't a philosopher and, as such, could not be qualified for being a man-ocean. He worked only on borrowed philosophies and resources.

While Mao gathered and trained his inputs of revolution locally—men and material—Bose had looked up to outside powers for his men and material requirements. It was a great difference between the two.

Mao altered the culture and work ethics of the Chinese people. His long march, Cultural Revolution and Red Guards were unique. Like Lenin, Mao infused a class struggle that first destroyed a lot that looked undesirable, and then built equivalently well, or even better.

He cleansed the Chinese society of bourgeois elements, or made them hide themselves. Bose's priority wasn't changing the Indian society. His first and the foremost desire was to see his Mother India freed from occupation by the British imperialists. Had he lived longer, then possibly on getting hold of levers of power in independent India, he would have attempted cleansing the Indian society of some evils like communalism, gender discrimination, caste divisions, and dowry etc.

Poonam Surie[6] in her recent work titled '**China: Confucius in Shadows**' said, as under, about the great chairman of the Chinese people:

> *"It is said that Mao was an ascetic and a very intense, shy and extremely serious person. His instance was to lean towards the common*

> *man and the layperson rather than towards the elite. A brilliant strategist yet simple, wily yet humble. The sheer brilliance of the man makes him stand out as an icon even today, in spite of a thousand issues and opinions about him in China and indeed all over the world."*

In terms of iconic perceptions, Bose isn't far behind Mao. And, as far as issues and opinions are concerned, he enjoys a serious load of controversies in India as well as abroad too. While Bose's fan following is primarily limited to India and some East Asian regions, Mao attained a worldwide spread of fans and followers.

Since Bose had no time for working through his people, there wasn't any chance for him to change them effectively. And unlike Mao, he could leave no significant legacies for people of the world to appreciate and follow.

Mao was a destroyer of old traditions and superstitions; the tradition of binding of women's feet was halted at his direction. His anti-Confucianism and talk of science changed the outlook of Chinese generations. He laid foundations of China becoming an industrial, economic and military superpower.

And Mao had a team of committed followers who took his revolutionary ideas and practices to fruitful heights—which unfortunately wasn't the case with Bose. The large Bose family, too, couldn't throw out any significant and/or a worthy follower of the great revolutionary.

On the *'scale of strength of purpose'*, Bose fared well with Mao; both had superior strength of objectivity. But with regard to diplomatic skills, Bose was much ahead of Mao. He had travelled a lot more and interacted with several leaders of Axis powers and its command functionaries.

Mao primarily limited himself to his own *karamchetra*, and his sense of purpose was so strong that many people lined-up for appointments with him. Nixon and Kissinger came on bent knees for an audience with the great leader.

As a generator of new thoughts and ensuring their acceptance by people, there has been no comparison of Mao Zedong. Here, not Bose but Gandhi offered stronger, or rather better comparison. Gandhi's ideas of non-violence travelled far and wide; they still have massive applicability as far as welfare of people and world peace is concerned.

Mao founded the Communist Party of China (CPC); in fact, his life was consumed in creating and nursing the party, making it a great institution. Bose, too, had founded the Forward Bloc—initially as a pressure group within Congress which later was turned into a separate political party, but he didn't nurture it as Mao did his CPC. And result of the two approaches were clearly seen through their subsequent roles in respective nations' growth. While CPC turned China into a superpower, Subhash's Forward Block faded into insignificance.

Mao was a poet and a writer; his Red Book has been an iconic work. Bose, too, wrote his autobiography; but the two works have never been comparable.

Mao had a strong desire to coerce nature into obedience[6] as he once commented:

"Make the high mountain bow its head; make the river yield its way."

His love for control and grandiose schemes was evidenced by projects such as the construction of the Three Gorges Dam across the river Yangtze. It didn't matter if the project subsequently turned into an environmental liability, or a disaster.

Mao's strategy for dominance, "**the countryside surrounding the cities**", and then creating bases where the Red Army and Communist Party would grow strong was indeed unique. Bose, on the other, hadn't mastered such fine nuances of war and winning. His approach was dictated by his Axis power masters.

Looking deeply, one finds that Bose believed in the strategy of dominance too—but he applied it only in meetings and conferences. As a Congress president in late 1930s, he attempted to dominate the whole Congress organization—he even challenged Gandhiji's approach to means and methods of agitation, economic development, industrialization and rural transformation.

It didn't work.

Mahatma Gandhi wasn't made of stuff that could easily yield to the game of dominance. His thoughts were deep, and his action rested on well-experimented approach.

Mao's principle[6] was that the party commands the gun, and the gun must never be allowed to command the party. His military tactics were those of guerilla warfare:

> *"The enemy advance, we retreat. The enemy halts, we harass. The enemy withdraws, we attack. The enemy retreats, we pursue."*

Mao had learnt from Sunzi's (Sun Tze's) *Art of War* and fine-tuned his strategies during the war-filled years. Throughout the bitterly difficult period of the '***Long March***' he had stressed that the communists should not show any vacillation on the matter of principle. In a way, Mao's achievements as a revolutionary, social reformer and a political heavy weight were superior to even those of Lenin from whom, at least initially, he had learnt some basic ropes of creating and managing a revolution.

Che Guevara and Fidel Castro

Ernesto R. Guevara was born in a middle class family in Rosario, Argentina, on June 14, 1928. He studied medicine before travelling around South America, observing conditions of people that spurred his Marxist beliefs. He concluded that solution to poverty and exploitation in South American countries rested in spread of Marxist revolution.

Guevara first became politically active in his native Argentina, and then in neighbouring Bolivia and Guatemala. In 1954, he met Cuban revolutionary Fidel Castro and his brother Raul while in Mexico. Guevara became part of Fidel Castro's efforts to overthrow the dictatorial Batista, who was ruthless in exploiting Cuban people. The young Guevara was a frontline fighter. He later engaged in guerrilla action in Bolivia, where he was killed. He's revered by many as a cultural hero.

Castro overthrew Batista in 1959, and took over power in Cuba. From 1959-1961, Guevara was the president of the National Bank of Cuba, and then minister of industry. In this position, he travelled the world as an ambassador of Cuba. At home, he carried out plans for land re-distribution and the nationalisation of industry.

A strong opponent of the United States, he guided the country towards alignment with the Soviet Union. The Cuban economy faltered as a result of American trade sanctions and unsuccessful Marxist reforms. During this difficult time, Guevara began to fall out with other Cuban leaders. He later expressed his desire to spread revolution in other parts of the developing world, and in 1965, Castro announced that Guevara had left Cuba.

Guevara then spent several months in Africa, particularly the Congo, attempting to train rebel forces in guerrilla warfare. His efforts failed, and in 1966, he secretly returned to Cuba. From Cuba, he travelled to Bolivia to lead forces rebelling against the government of René Barrientos Ortuño. With US assistance, the Bolivian Army captured Guevara. And along with some of his fighters, the great revolutionary was executed on October 9, 1967 in the Bolivian village of La Higuera. His body was buried in a secret location. In 1997, his remains were discovered, exhumed and returned to Cuba, where he was reburied with due honour.

Like Mao, Che Guevara, was a Marxist revolutionary, guerrilla leader and a military theorist. Additionally, he was a physician and a diplomat. His objective of revolution wasn't limited to one country. And after his death, he rightly belonged to the whole of Latin America. He didn't seem limited to corner a territory for himself and/or his family.

There were large scale differences between lives of Guevara and that of Subhash Bose as well.

Guevara's life story became cause of several movies which still motivates masses the world over. Bose wasn't a trained military man. For the purpose of personality acceleration, he had adopted military uniform, but the difference between real and unreal never disappeared.

Fidel Castro

Fidel Castro, a modern world's nationalist and revolutionary of repute, had lot of early life similarities with Subhash Bose. He was born in August

1926, third in a six children's family (three brothers and same number of sisters) of a wealthy sugarcane planter.

Like Bose, Fidel was educated in private missionary schools too, but he didn't hate the Christian educators as there was no clash of religious formations.

He grew up in wealthy circumstances amid the poverty of Cuban people. He was intellectually gifted, but was more interested in sports than studies. He attended El Colegio de Belen and pitched for the school's baseball team. After his graduation in late 1945, Castro entered law school at the University of Havana, and became immersed in the political climate of Cuban nationalism, anti-imperialism and socialism. He was greatly influenced by Marxist ideals.

In 1959, Castro used guerilla warfare to successfully overthrow Cuban leader Batista, a capitalist dictator. Che Guevara had assisted him in throwing away the Cuban dictator. And after the victory, Castro was sworn in as the Prime Minister of Cuba. As Cuban PM, Castro's government established covert military and economic relations with the Soviet Union, leading to the Cuban Missile Crisis. He served as PM until 1976, when he became the President of Cuba. Later, he handed state control to his brother Raul Castro.

Fidel Castro exhibited intellectual capacity as was evident from his quotes such as:

> *"A revolution is a struggle to the death between the future and the past";*
> *"Capitalism is using its money; we socialists throw it away" and.*
> *"I think that a man should not live beyond the age when he begins to deteriorate, when the flame that lighted the brightest moment of his life has weakened."*

Contrary to the above quote, Fidel is living an old age. And finally, he and his brother in the 2nd decade of the 21st century successfully steered their nation to reconcile with the long-term adversary, the United State of America.

Mustafa Kemal Ataturk

Mustafa Kemal Ataturk was a Turkish army officer who turned revolutionary, and became the President of modern Turkey. He is credited with being the founder of the Republic of Turkey.

He was a nationalist of high order, and Subhash Bose was impressed with his personality and the no-nonsense methods that he employed for ruling Turkey and transforming it into a modern non-Islamic state.

Mustafa Kemal Ataturk was born in 1881 (16 years before Subhash Bose) in Salonika (now Thessaloniki) in what was then the Ottoman Empire. His father was a minor official and later a timber merchant. Ataturk studied in a military school and military academy in Istanbul, graduating in 1905.

In early 1910s, he fought against the Italians in Libya and then in the Balkan Wars (1912-1913). His military reputation skyrocketed when forces under his command repelled the Allied invasion at the Dardanelles in 1915.

In May 1919, resisting the peace settlement imposed on Turkey by the victorious Allies, Ataturk began a nationalist revolution in Anatolia. It was particularly focused on resisting Greek attempts to seize some Turkish territories, and the victory over the Greeks enabled him to secure revision of the peace settlement in the Treaty of Lausanne.

In 1921, He established a provisional government in Ankara and in the following year, he formally abolished the Ottoman Sultanate. In 1923, he turned Turkey into a secular republic with himself as its President. He established a single party regime that lasted almost without interruption until 1945.

Also, he launched a programme of revolutionary social and political reforms for correcting social ills of the Turkish society, which subsequently led to modernisation of the new Turkey. He established friendly relations with Turkey's neighbours—including the former adversaries. Further, through these reforms, he ensured emancipation of women, the abolition of all Islamic institutions and the introduction of Western legal codes, dress, calendar and alphabet, replacing the Arabic script with a Latin one. It was indeed a great achievement, and young Bose appreciated his actions, policies and the authoritarian methods of his working.

In 1935, he was given the name of *Ataturk*, meaning '***Father of the Turks***'. .He died in November 1938. He remains hero of the Turkish people.

Like many other revolutionaries of the present times, Ataturk depended upon local resources and worked through and with his own people. That, probably, was the influence of his military training. He fought, at different times, against the fascists of Italy as well as the allied powers. Successfully steering his country during the difficult years of WW I and coming out in good shape wasn't a small achievement.

Subhash Bose appreciated Ataturk's nationalism but couldn't copy his methodology.

Charles de Gaulle

Charles André Joseph Marie de Gaulle was a French general who had the rare distinction of participating in both the World Wars of the 20th century. He was a resistant fighter, a writer and a statesman of repute. Like Subhash Bose, he was a nationalist of high order. And unlike Bose, he was a trained military man.

Besides being a general and a statesman, De Gaulle was the leader of the Free French struggle during World War II and the architect of the Fifth Republic. His political ideology, 'Gaullism', become a major influence in French politics.

Charles de Gaulle was born in Lille on November 22, 1890 and grew up in Paris, where his father was a teacher. De Gaulle chose a military career and saw active action in World War I, and spent time in a prisoners of war camp too.

He was a forceful advocate of strong defence on the northern borders with Germany. During the 1930s, he wrote books and articles on military subjects, criticising France's reliance on the Maginot Line for defence, and advocated the formation of mechanised armoured columns. His advice was ignored and as a result, in June 1940, German forces took no time in over-running France. As in-charge of national defence and war, de Gaulle refused to accept the French government's truce with the Germans and escaped to London, where he announced the formation of a French government in exile.

He became leader of the Free French.

This was the greatest similarity between Bose and the great French nationalist.

After liberation of France in August 1944, de Gaulle was given a hero's welcome in Paris. As President of the provisional government, he spearheaded writing of the French Constitution—on which the Fourth Republic was based. But when his desires for a strong presidency were not met, he resigned in 1953, and withdrew into temporary retirement.

Algerian war complications in 1958, combined with serious instability within France, destroyed the Fourth Republic. On public demand, De Gaulle returned to lead France once again. A strong new constitution was prepared, and the great nationalist was voted President of the Fifth Republic. Strongly nationalistic, de Gaulle sought to strengthen his country financially and militarily. He did take several strong and unpopular decisions like sanctioning development of nuclear weapons, withdrawal of France from NATO and vetoing the entry of Britain into the Common Market. He also granted independence to Algeria in the face of strong opposition at home, and from French settlers in Algeria.

He handled students' revolt in May 1968 with a strong hand. Although the Fifth Republic was shaken, De Gaulle held elections and the country rallied behind him, ending the crisis. In April 1969, De Gaulle resigned the presidency after losing a referendum on a reform proposal. He retired to his estate at Colombey-les-Deux-Eglises, and died of a heart attack on 9 November 1970.

French people loved de Gaulle as much as Indians loved Subhash Bose. His performance in national defence and nation building was unique—while Bose had made hugely popular promises to the Indian people but never really delivered.

Gandhi and Mandela

Mahatma Gandhi was the greatest non-violent revolutionary that the world has ever seen. He had worked in South Africa as a peaceful Satyagrahist, before returning to India in 1915. Mandela and his African National Congress (ANC) had learnt from Gandhi how to peacefully defeat mighty racially discriminating regimes.

Unlike Bose, neither Gandhi nor his great disciple Mandela looked for outside help for defeating their political adversaries.

Nelson Rolihlahla Mandela was a South African anti-apartheid revolutionary, politician and philanthropist, who served as the President of South Africa from 1994 to 1999. The vicious system of apartheid that he and his colleagues fought in South Africa was more deeply entrenched and cruel to the black majority than what Subhash Bose and his Forward Bloc followers experienced in India.

He was born as Rolihlahla Mandela in 1918 into the Madiba clan in the village of Mvezo in South Africa, and his father Nkosi Mphakanyiswa Gadla Mandela worked as principal counsellor to the acting King of the Thembu people. In 1930, when he was 12 years old, his father died. The young Rolihlahla became a ward of Jongintaba at the Great Place in Mqhekezweni.[1]

Hearing from elders' stories of his ancestors' valour during the wars of resistance, he dreamed also of making his own contribution to the freedom struggle of his people. Like Bose, Mandela was drawn into nationalistic struggle at an early age too. But he didn't turn to violent methods despite the fact that the African society was more violence-oriented than the Indian society. He also didn't look for outside help for furthering his struggle.

He attended primary school in Qunu where his teacher gave him the name Nelson, in accordance with the custom of giving all school children Christian names. He joined ANC's quest for freedom from apartheid through its youth wing.

In June 1964, Mandela and seven other accused—Walter Sisulu, Ahmed Kathrada, Govan Mbeki, Raymond Mhlaba, Denis Goldberg,

Elias Motsoaledi and Andrew Mlangeni—were convicted and sentenced to life imprisonment. Goldberg was sent to Pretoria Prison because he was white, while the others went to Robben Island.

He was released from prison on 11 February 1990, nine days after the unbanning of the ANC. Throughout his imprisonment; he had rejected at least three conditional offers of release. He didn't seek any foreign assistance for freeing people of South Africa from the evil of white minority rule. ANC was like Congress in India, and followed mostly the non-violent Gandhian principles of agitation.

Mandela held rigorous dialogue with the minority rulers to end white minority rule and in 1991, was elected ANC President to replace his ailing friend, Oliver Tambo. In 1993, he and President FW de Klerk jointly won the Nobel Peace Prize and on 27 April 1994, he voted for the first time in his life. On 10 May 1994, he was inaugurated as South Africa's first democratically elected President. He married three times and had several children.

True to his promise, Mandela stepped down in 1999 after one term as President. He continued to work with the Nelson Mandela Children's Fund he set up in 1995 and established the Nelson Mandela Foundation and The Mandela Rhodes Foundation.

Nelson Mandela never wavered in his devotion to democracy, equality and learning. Despite terrible provocations, he never answered racism with racism. His life is an inspiration to all who are oppressed and deprived; and to all who are opposed to oppression and deprivation.

He died at his home in Johannesburg on December 5, 2013.

He was a worthy disciple of a great guru Mahatma Gandhi.

Coming to conclusion with regard to Subhash Bose's place amongst revolutionaries of present times, one can reasonably conclude:

On account of strength of purpose, motivation, expertise and diplomatic skills, Bose performed fairly well. His commitment towards India's freedom from the imperialistic British was indeed great. He motivated his soldiers well, but failed on resource planning and strategy on the war front. His diplomatic skills were decidedly incomparable. In terms of localization of revolution and people's involvement, he was substantially off the mark. Except the energies of nationalism, the ideology and content of his struggle wasn't distinctively impressive.

Jai Hind

SECTION II

FICTIONAL ACCOUNT

Subhash Bose's life has been a strange mix of facts and fiction—and after August 1945 twists of the WW II, it became difficult to separate the two aspects. It is particularly hard on his fans and admirers whether to accept the plane crash theory or to dream and decode his secret life in the wilderness of Siberia, in its desolate jails or gulags—or in the dusty plains of north India.

These scenarios were unpleasant and deeply unsettling for the great revolutionary's fans and admirers. It was even more upsetting to realize that our great advocate of use of violent means to free India from the imperialistic grip of the British made numerous promises and predictions for the people of India—but none of the same came to be true. It made the fictional aspect of the great Subhash Bose's story more relevant and satisfying to his fans' psyche. In the next two chapters of this work, an attempt is made to explore and understand the same.

Subhash Bose's fans and admirers had a lot of expectations from him. As the post-independence democratic India progressed on the development front—and over the years, bureaucracy and corruption took hold of the administration at all levels—Bose's fans and admires' frustrations and longing skyrocketed. Many people fell into dream situations about their legendry revolutionary hero on a fictional plane.

They theorized and hoped:

> *"If Bose had survived and had taken over as the Prime Minister of India, the country would have become a heaven of efficiency and productivity."*

The two chapters under this section deal with the fictional longings of his ardent fans and admirers.

Chapter 11 deals with the dream of the great hero's fans when they see him as the first Prime Minister of India. It details the shape and form that the country would have taken under the efficient but mercurial persona of Subhash Bose.

Chapter 12 details a purely fictional dialogue between a deeply frustrated fan of the great revolutionary and the divine soul as it is forced by the love of the former to come and answer queries and mollify the disturbed fan.

CHAPTER 11

BOSE AS PRIME MINISTER INDIA

Many Indians—Bengalis and non-Bengalis, intellectuals and simpletons—often opine that Subhash Chandra Bose would have been a better Prime Minister for independent India. It has been an earnest dream or an unfulfilled desire of the great revolutionary's innumerable fans and admirers. This perception, right or wrong, primarily sprouted out of the following factors or thought formations:

- Firstly, people normally have more favourable orientation towards what hasn't been seen and/or experienced. Because an untested regime or individual gets the benefit of non-performance, his or her deficiencies and faults not having been visible or experienced—and hence, the same do not cloud thoughts and expectations of people. It is normally imaginary in nature, yet it doesn't stop from emerging on the thought canvas of people. For Indian people, expectations from Bose have been an un-tasted fruit that, due to uncontrollable circumstances, didn't come their way.
- Secondly, negative manifestations of incumbency for a ruler or administrator, democratic or otherwise, are often impossible to avoid. As an indispensable rule, performance tends to magnify deficiencies of commission and omission. The long rule of Congress in India activated negativities of non-Congress elements, and many Congress components that didn't get the

opportunity to grab national resources in the exploitable democratic environment—or those who were caught in such deviant acts—became progressively unhappy. Leaders do generate jealousy among their followers when they miss opportunity for self-aggrandizement. Eventually—through various means—they strive for grabbing levers of power, forming new parties and alliances and exploiting caste, class and religious differences in the society. The battle between haves and have-nots, too, accelerated as economic development in the country gained pace.

- In so doing, they found it convenient to criticize Congress in general and Jawaharlal Nehru in particular. For the past five decades or so, Nehru hasn't been here to defend himself, and his party-men attempted to defend the organization and /or the Gandhi-Nehru family only very meekly.
- Subhash Bose's impact on the psyche of Indian public, without exception, has been deep and intense. Disgruntled elements from groups such as Ambedkerites, backwards and dalits, communists, Hindutva adherents, Forward Blocists, Dravidians and Alkalis, just to name a few, impatiently strived to get ahead in the race of political power appropriation. And in the process, considerations of region, caste, class and/or religion turned deep and substantial indeed. Bose's influence didn't evaporate with time, thanks to his death/or disappearance myth and mysteries which were kept alive vigorously by the renowned Bose family on one hand, and his innumerable fans, on the other. They waited listlessly for return of the great hero. Did this contribute, in some way, towards the present-day irritability of some sections of Indians (primarily politicians) towards the Gandhi-Nehru family? Or is it the insecurity of the non-performers and the unscrupulous against those who performed almost selflessly?
- In the second decade of the 21st century, BJP and the Hindutva elements' efforts to attain power at the Center became intense and in 2014, they succeeded in replacing the Congress-led UPA. But the conquest wasn't wide enough over the geographic canvas of the democratic India—and the lack of the NDA's majority in the upper house of the Parliament pushed them to add more states under their bandwagon. In these efforts, they unabashedly

> attempted to appropriate and own some prominent icons of India's freedom struggle, thinking of that tactic as a smart way of grabbing votes. Starting with Sardar Patel, they tried to appropriate Ambadekar, Lal Bahadur Shastri and Rajendera Prasad—and when time came for campaigning in Eastern India—they couldn't resist the temptation of grabbing the legacy of Subhash Bose either. In this effort, the renowned Bose family became a willing accomplice, and the drama of declassifying the Bose files was a massive culmination of the process. Both sides looked for benefiting from extractions of the great leader's legacy. As per their theories and beliefs, Subhash hadn't died in a plane crash but escaped into the Russian wilderness—and nobody bothered for when the aged hero needed help during his self-imposed *sanyas* in central Asia or in the dilapidated central Uttar Pradesh. They were only interested to extract maximum emotional benefits from his fans' vote bank.

Had Bose won the battles of Imphal and Kohima and pushed deeper into Eastern India, or had he and his key commanders of his INA gone deep into the jungles on the Indo- Burma border and taken to guerrilla warfare instead of taking a flight to the Japanese Capital (or wherever)—and if he was around at the auspicious occasion of India's independence—there sure is no doubt that he could have easily assumed the charge of guiding the destiny of India (and possibly also that of Pakistan). He had considerable support within the Congress party, and his own '***Forward Bloc***' was there to support him in all possible ways too. And in that situation, he would have had a great chance of experimenting with his ideas, philosophies and energies for turning India into a great power.

Bose's Path of Choice: Socialism or Communism?

His ideals of socialism were deep—but normally, facts are different than fiction. And hence, would the great leader have adhered to his ideals of socialism, or turned communist, seeing and experiencing difficulties in managing a great mass of people that a poverty and shortages-stricken India of that time might have caused him to face?

And in democracy, keeping all sections of people—especially the more vocal and demanding kind— or keeping the vote banks satisfied, is not easy. So, in that situation with his inherent tendencies of authoritarianism, would he not have turned dictatorial? His exposure to fascism and fascists was substantial. In the enormous literature that is available on the great leader, at places, he has been reported to have stressed the need for dictatorship for the first 20 years in the post-independence period for the purpose of avoiding post-revolution chaotic situations—as had engulfed France after its famous revolution of 1879. And in that case, India would have competed with Pakistan, which faced several dictators after its birth in 1947.

Under Bose's dictatorship, would India have fared better than Pakistan did, or what people of Cuba and China suffered for decades? It is, today, a purely hypothetical formation. But those who missed independent India being ruled by Subhash Bose must ponder deeply about it as the possibility of such a situation wasn't fully theoretical.

Economic Development

Industrial development was dear to both Bose and Nehru. In fact, the former's differences with Gandhi originated out of airing of his views on industrialization, which went against the Gandhian model of development. And on the contentious issue, in Congress' internal debates, Nehru sided with Bose. In Congress circles, the two emerging young leaders were acclaimed leftists of the 1920s and 1930s. Hence, it can be said with substantial certainty that had Bose been at the helm of affairs of India in the post-independence era, the industrial development in the country, most likely, might have moved faster than what actually happened under Nehru's stewardship.

How much faster?

It's difficult to extrapolate with the help of available information. Technical assistance from Germany, Japan and even from Soviet Union would have been smoother than what happened under Nehru's premiership—and the same might have contributed to better and/or faster development.

And there was another possibility!

Under socialistic push and on having been impressed with what Soviet Russia had achieved during its first 4-5 post-revolution decades, India would have followed the same path too. And, as a final scenario, the whole of India—like West Bengal—could have turned into an industrial graveyard. That the communist governance and its labour activists during the pre-Trinamool decades had pushed industrialists and businessmen out of West Bengal is a well-documented fact. Why wouldn't have such a situation prevailed at a much wider arena under Bose's rule can't be said to be a matter of pure imagination?

Military Affairs and Defense

Military affairs were Bose's forte, and hence, India definitely would have done much better militarily under Bose's leadership. All soldiers and commandants of the INA would have been at his command—most of them would have been absorbed into the post-independence Indian Army. And in that case, there possibly would have been no 1962 fiasco on the Indo-China border. But it is also uncertain how Mao Zedong, a great military genius, would have interacted with Bose who was an active ally of the Japanese—the tormentors of Chinese people in 1930s—-and till the defeat of the Axis powers in 1945.

On the Western front, Pakistan most probably wouldn't have dared to send tribesmen (or regulars dressed as tribals) into the Kashmir valley. And in case the folly of covert invasion was committed, with the known military expertise of Bose on our side, Kashmir issue possibly wouldn't have taken the present shape.

But in subsequent years, British and US support to Pakistan would sure have been more active because of their long standing antagonism with Bose. And with the Bengali restiveness against the West Pakistani exploitation and discrimination, 1971 war which culminated into birth of Bangladesh, would sure have come much earlier.

International Relations and Cold War

One thing seems sure though: that in the event of Bose having become the first PM of independent India, there would have been no Commonwealth. British would have found it difficult to align with their ex-enemy. And with that, at least in the initial period, India's relations with the Western world would have been frosty, if not wholly hostile.

Non-alignment that Nehru cultivated so rigorously as a tool of India's foreign policy would have, for sure, not seen light of the day under our great revolutionary's premiership.

Cold War scenario of the first few decades of the post WW II period possibly wouldn't have been much different, as on account of Bose's socialist/communist orientation, aligning with the Soviet bock wouldn't have been difficult. Rather, it would have been a default path, or a natural choice under Bose's Prime Minister-ship.

Khadi and Rural Development

Surely, rural development and Khadi would have taken a different turn. Fans of Bose, instead of Gandhi's followers, would have been in the limelight on our political and bureaucratic arenas—manning and managing all developmental and non-developmental institutions of free India. With little Khadi and no Gandhi cap, most of the corrupt politicians would have found it difficult to take holistic cover of the white Khadi.

Most of them, possibly, would have taken to donning unauthorized and uncomfortable military uniforms on their disproportionate potbellies!

Bose had talked about socializing and radicalizing the rural developmental scene of India. And hence, much like the Soviet Union—with collectivization of farming or Mao's Cultural Revolution—sufferings of our rural folks would have been intense and long-lasting. And possibly, there would have been no '***Green Revolution***' the advent of which in India was facilitated with a lot of western help.

Communal Harmony

Would communal harmony with Bose at the top have assumed some different form than what happened under the long Congress rule? Or would he have persuaded the Muslim League to be less insistent with its two-nation theory? Or in post-partition days, would it have had a change of heart and rejoined India as a federation or under some other arrangement?

The author is, however, sure that with Bose being around, the number of communal riots in independent India would have been much smaller in number and frequency. There would have been no need to coerce anyone to raise slogans such as '***Bharat Mata ki Jai***'.

And there would have been no reason for the beef eaters to fear for their lives as the great revolutionary himself was known to enjoy animal-based delicacies.

And in that situation, one could never be sure about the possibility of NDA to have taken birth in this land. And what about the RSS: would it have grown to its present shape?

And then there is another surety: we would have had no opportunity for a '***chaiwalla***' to become PM of India in the post-Bose century.

Food and Agricultural Development

At the time of gaining independence, India was a country of perplexing shortages—almost everything starting from food grains, sugar, cloth, kerosene, medicines and fertilizers to cement, just to name a few things, was under controlled supply. We weren't producing enough of almost anything (except malnourished babies). British, in their drive to promote their own goods had suffocated Indian manufacturing—small as well as large scale ones. We were rich only in diseases and poverty.

For import of food, for feeding its hungry millions, whom would the Bose government have turned to? Germany, Japan and Russia—all had suffered the crushing war-induced food shortages. Only United States of America, Canada and Australia had enough surplus food that could help India—as USA actually did under the PL-480 scheme in the 1960s through 1970s. Would Bose have put enough resources into agricultural research and rural development, and caused an impressive '***Green Revolution***' faster than what Nehru-Gandhi regimes did with imported seeds, fertilizers and pesticides?

For sure, we don't know.

But wouldn't the Bengal and Bihar-type famines occurring in greater frequency and with wider spread be a greater possibility in case of India having come under Bose and his fans' rule after independence?

We don't know with any certainty!

Intensity of Corruption

Today, it is easy to presume that under Bose's governance corruption wouldn't have grown to the present-day obnoxious levels. But energies of power are strange—they tend to corrupt almost everyone; exceptions are decidedly few and far between. How Bose would have controlled the great mass of his fans and admirers—and also the large and ambitious Bose family from striving to actively grab spoils of power and economic development? It sure wouldn't have been easy.

Bose, with his military-oriented government, wouldn't have done away with arms-agents. And the intensity of 'Sarada' and 'Narada' scams wouldn't have been remarkably different.

Danger of Dynastic Rule

Political dynasties are not uncommon. In India, every state has suffered dynastic proliferations. In states like Uttar Pradesh, Bihar, Punjab, Haryana, Odisha and Tamil Nadu, second and third generations of dynasties are strangulating the economies of suffering states. And there, in fact, is no state in the Indian Union that is wholly free from the malice of dynastic rule.

Taking a worldview, dictators are more prone to creating damaging dynasties than what is the situation in case of democracies. Our Nehru-Gandhi dynasty directly ruled for over three decades, and then its indirect influence continued for another two decades or so. This happened when

Jawaharlal Nehru, India's first Prime Minister, had only one child. The small family established a dynasty that the politicians of present-day India don't stop complaining about endlessly. Now, let us imagine the situation that we might have landed ourselves into if Subhash Bose, with an over-three-dozen-strong extended family—which was politically active right in the pre-independence days—had taken over as India's first PM. It is difficult to foresee how a large crop of nephews and nieces (and later the grand ones) could have been prevented from taking advantage of the situation—grabbing levers of power in deserving as well as non-deserving manner.

In that event, would our Janta brigade or the socialists of myriad hues and/or NDA components—its poets and chaiwallas alike—have had any chance to taste power of governance? It would have been highly unlikely.

Four Likely Scenarios

All the above formations today are a matter of conjecture and thought warriorism. And it is prudent not to indulge into too much of kite-flying and say and/or presume that Bose as the first PM of India, instead of Nehru, would have worked miracles. He sure didn't have a magic wand with him!

It wouldn't have been possible for Subhash Bose to follow British-styled democracy in India. The long antipathy that he held towards the British was sure to have come in the way. He hated Americans equally deeply. His Waterloo at the Indo–Burma border, to a considerable extent, was dictated by the US Air Force support to the allied forces pitched against his INA and its Nipponese masters.

In brief, under Bose's stewardship as India's first P M and, after him someone from the large Bose family, would have undoubtedly taken over to further his legacies and schemes, India would have suffered one of the following four political scenarios:

- With his penchant of military approach for solving problems, a Pakistan-type situation wouldn't have been wholly unlikely. Bose's style was working for and through dominance. He wasn't a man of consensus; as a leader, he needed to be followed.

- A Myanmar-type of military-dictated governance could possibly have been our next best choice. With Bose at the top, no government would possibly have had a chance for democratic operations. Sometimes, for quick decision making and faster results, democracy becomes a hindrance. And did Bose possess adequate patience for democratic working? But let us not forget if good results can be achieved otherwise, there is no sacredness for democracy or head of a government being a consensus man.
- Bose was a celebrated leftist right from his Congress days. Through the route of socialism and communism, he had travelled into the company of fascism and had stayed with it for whole of his last phase of life. Since the need for arms and food was great in the early years of India's independence, Soviet Union-type governance for India was another great possibility under the coveted stewardship of Subhash Bose.
- As a country ruled by a known anti-West revolutionary, India's post-independence fate could also have been similar to that of Fidel Castro's Cuba. But did Bose have the perseverance of Castro? The author, on various counts, finds it highly unlikely.

For the admirers and fans of Netaji, it won't be easy to proceed if they are today asked to make a choice.

Jai Hind

CHAPTER 12

LAMENTATIONS OF A FAN OF NETAJI

Every morning, an ardent fan of Subhash Bose stood in front of his hero's photograph(a poster cutout) hanging on a dust-laden wall of a dwelling in a village located on bank of the Ganga canal in Western Uttar Pradesh. He offered silent prayers to his great hero. This fan of Bose was a regular at the *Prabhat Pheries* (or morning rounds) of the pre-independence era and raised loudest slogans, the center-piece of which happened to be: **Netaji Zindabad***!*

Often, he was the loudest. And his friends and colleagues respected his feelings and energy of patriotism.

Every day, a group of young boys from the village walked together to and fro their school located in a nearby town, some five miles each way. Those days, it wasn't considered a long distance and the boys often ran through the whole distance, a dusty bullock carts' track, with the ease of a long-distance professional.

Sometimes, while raiding guava orchards on way back and on finding some good fruits, they spontaneously shouted the well-practiced slogans. In mid 1940s, it was a freedom-filled atmosphere in rural India. The few old men who kept watch for the Nawab's orchards preferred to look the other way. Firstly, they were students; their number was large and the

Nawab, right a year in advance of partition, had run away to the North West Frontier areas that were finally included in the newly-formed Pakistan. There was no logic for the orchard watchmen in resisting the otherwise harmless boys. Additionally, in the independence-soaked environment, the keepers of the orchards felt good in letting the boys enjoy nature's gift.

In the school, teachers, too, were in independence-soaked atmosphere; they won't entertain any complaint against their students. Pandit Bhola Nath, the head master of the school, was a great fan of Netaji. He often encouraged students to raise slogans in appreciation of freedom fighters, and often distributed sweets at his own expense.

The boys loved him.

He had special love for Netaji and didn't mind reminding his pupils that the great hero had promised ***"Delhi Chalo"***.

He often said:

> *"Netaji will soon reach the Red Fort where his INA soldiers and their commanders were facing a court marshal."*

Students believed whatsoever the Masterji said. And other teachers of the primary school didn't contradict their senior. The school had vibrant atmosphere that could possibly be seen only in a freedom fighters' camp.

Time passed at its own pace. Students moved to higher classes but the head master waited for his hero to emerge in Delhi. A few times a year, almost once in three months, he secretly made a visit to Delhi and devotedly went to the Red Fort to be sure whether there was any symptom of his great hero's visit to the historic structure. His enthusiasm was electric and expectation great. It was, in a way, an ardent lover's journey to meet his hero. He didn't mind the great effort and the expenses incurred on such journeys.

But, every time, he returned disappointed. Although the headmaster kept his visits secret, his students could see the disappointment on his face. Like many other Indians, he hadn't accepted the August 1945 plane crash theory on death/or disappearance of the great revolutionary. He was sure that his hero had escaped through disguise, and would soon be in Delhi. Some senior students, once in a while, went to the Panditji to check whether he had some news and more reliable information on the great national hero.

By 1957, a decade past the great event of gaining independence, we (the Masterji's senior students) started noticing that everything wasn't OK with the middle-aged headmaster. He seemed to have descended into depression and took to self-talking, asking questions loudly and getting agitated on not being satisfied. It was a dialogue between a fan and the soul of his hero.

Often, he was seen standing in a dilapidated classroom, in front of blackboard and, as he was used to, asked questions as if he was conducting a class. In fact, he talked to his great hero's soul—often complaining loudly. Sometimes, some of us hid ourselves under back benches of the classroom and, without making any noise, attempted to decipher what the Masterji said.

We concluded that he was disappointed with his hero. In fact, he was angry and, except abusing directly, he employed all possible hard words and phrases attempting to talk to his hero and extract some replies and/or assurances. He raised questions one by one and for each case, he waited for a brief moment—and then answered as if it was his hero talking through him and attempting to calm the agitated fan. For the Masterji, his hero was under examination and he must answer all of what was asked.

One of Masterji's loyal students had noted the dialogue of a possessed fan with his hero's soul. It was secured into two hardcover note-books for long time preservation. Once in a while, the said student (when he grew up and assumed family responsibilities) took out the notebooks, dusted them lovingly and read and re-read the divine dialogue in complete solitude.

As years passed, Masterji's mental condition deteriorated. And it was heard that one evening, he jumped into the Ganga canal, because satisfying replies were not coming forth from his hero.

He couldn't tolerate the pain of his hero having failed him. He felt cheated. And his students felt bad.

A few years before, Masterji's wife who was addressed by us as Masterni, had committed suicide by jumping in the same canal too. She was tormented by her mother-in-law, i.e. Masterji's mother—and desired to go to the Brahamloka and be with her own mother. Masterji, although a local leader widely consulted by people, couldn't persuade women of the house to observe restraint. While students feared him, women of the household didn't care.

Decades passed, and in middle of the second decade of the 21st century when controversy about Netaji's death/ or disappearance mystery heated up during the NDA government's days of declassification of Bose files, Masterji's student took out the well-preserved note-books in which he had noted a long dialogue between Masterji as his hero's soul again. He sat under a neem tree and read the heritage books again, word by word.

The dialogue had gone as under:

"Subhash, I have gone to Delhi several times. I have searched all corners of the Red Fort. I saw several INA soldiers there but no trace of you. Tell me, why haven't you come to Delhi?" Masterji demanded angrily.

You had told us: ***"Delhi Chalo".***

"Everybody is there except you. I never thought you didn't bother to keep promises," shouted Masterji, upholding the Mulberry stick that he carried regularly.

For a moment, students hiding under the benches were scared but, fearing Masterji's stick, they kept silent. "We will get a good thrashing if Masterji finds out that we are listening to him hidden under the benches," whispered the leader of the group.

Everyone concurred, whispering back quietly but continued with the boyish mischief.

Now, in a mild tone, Masterji's hero responded:

"I was there Masterji! I saw you going around the great monument. Several times, I crossed your path. I wanted to touch you but I hesitated

for reasons of my ephemeral existence."

"I couldn't stop you—because my action would have been against the law of the Almighty," added the great hero's soul a bit boldly.

"You know Masterji... that celestial spy Narada, who keeps a watch on all the souls who are allowed temporarily to wander out of the Brahamloka, would have given out the secret of my meeting with you," added the hero's soul to convince his fan.

"I don't give a damn about Narada," responded Masterji.

"I like talking to you," said the great soul in an intervening effort, "Will come whenever you so desire," it promised hurriedly.

Masterji was mollified a little bit. His state of agitation cooled off by a few degrees.

"Subhash, my students wanted to see you. So many people waited for you. The whole country was looking for you to come and take over reins of the independent India as its first Prime Minister. We wanted to make you the first Prime Minister of India," Masterji elaborated ruefully.

A little more excited, the great fan now demanded:

"How did you go to the Brahamloka? Does disguise work there too? If that works, then I, too, want to come and be with you .I have a lot of things to clarify with you," said a slightly calming down Masterji.

"No, Masterji, you can't come here employing a disguise. The way to reach here is much more tedious. I came here through a plane ride that failed. I was going to Manchuria. I had plans to continue to fight for the freedom of India there from, possibly with Russian help." The great hero's soul attempted to explain.

"Well, my hero... I don't trust you anymore. You haven't kept your promise to your fans. I am greatly disappointed. People ask me questions about you and I can't answer. My position gets very delicate. I am a local leader; people respect me and call me Masterji. I can't even face my students any more. I am also going to take a plane ride from Delhi and reach you wherever you are," Masterji threatened while scribbling more queries on the blackboard.

"No, please don't!"

"Don't take the plane.".

"That is not the solution; tell me what do you want?" implored a greatly worried soul.

Masterji sensed an opportunity. His hero was in Brahamaloka's custody; he can't come here physically. And for him, going to the Brahamaloka wasn't easy. Yet he needed to be with his hero, as and when his urge overtook the senses. Being a wise teacher, he thought that he should extract some binding promises from his hero.

He demanded energetically:

> *"If you don't want me to come and join you in Brahamaloka, then you must come to my classroom, whenever I demand. I have to answer many people about the promises you made to all of us all through your years in India, in Europe and also in East Asia. You have escaped; I can't. So please accept my first demand," Masterji insisted.*

The great soul assessed the situation and understood the mess in which his fan had landed without any fault on his part.

"I couldn't keep the promises that I made in my raw enthusiasm—yet in case of Masterji, I need to do something special," the great soul argued with itself. "Masterji, your demand seems just; I will come to your classroom whenever you need me. Just write my name on the blackboard and make sure that no one else is there in the room," suggested the great hero's soul.

Masterji was delighted. He responded: "Yes, I will write your name 10 times instead of one. And I will be angry if you delay. But to ensure that no one else is in the room is beyond my control. My students are rowdy and they are skilled in disguise as well as in the art of hiding. So, please drop this part of the condition."

Reluctantly, the great hero's soul agreed.

By now, the great soul had been away from its station in Brahamaloka for a few Earth hours. There was danger to be detected; hence: "Will see you tomorrow same time. Then you raise all your questions," said the disappearing voice hurriedly.

Next day, Masterji looked a little refreshed. His *achkan* was well-ironed. And almost at the same time, as that of yesterday, he walked into the classroom. He taught the class for 45 minutes and when the school bell rang, all students were gone, except the group of five who went under the benches, without catching Masterji's eye. After cleaning the blackboard, Masterji wrote "Netaji" some 10 times with a crumbling chalk stick.

And within a minute, he bowed to the blackboard and started talking. His hero's soul, as promised, was there.

"I am glad that you have come. It is good to keep promises," Masterji said in a whisper.

"We have extreme poverty in the country. There isn't enough to eat and everything, except disease and rubbish, is in short supply. Sugar, cement, iron, dalda ghee, cloth and almost everything to sustain life is under control and one needs permit to buy," Masterji started with a long complaint. "And believe me; permits aren't easy to come by. One has to take the village Pardhan's certificate and go to the tehshel or block office, wait there for hours and often resort to bribing even for a chit of paper that allows you to buy a tin of dalda," lamented Masterji.

"You haven't come here to implement your socialism or dictatorship. How will situation improve under Nehru's mild leadership?" he demanded to know.

The great soul understood its fan's disquiet and attempted to put him at peace by saying:

> *"Look, Nehruji and I were colleagues in the Indian National Congress from 1923 to 1940. We were both leftists and collaborated on various policy and non-policy issues. He is a true socialist democrat. He isn't a communist and will never turn into a dictator. With me, there was a danger because I always wanted quick decisions and even quicker results. Nehru has more patience, and he is undoubtedly a capable leader. Further, he has assembled a good team of ministers and senior*

bureaucrats for development of the country."

Masterji, a deeply devoted fan, was mollified a bit but wasn't fully satisfied. He retorted:

> *"I know you are attempting to satisfy me. For me, a substitute can't ever be a good replacement. Were you here as PM, all of our youth, including my students would have joined the India Army, the INA. Their creative energies would have got a constructive direction. And all of us like the INA uniform. We could have been the strongest nation in the world, no?"*

Masterji's question was tough. The great hero's soul knew that it wasn't easy to satisfy a distraught fan. But the divine soul was under commitment to answer all queries of its fan. Hence, without delay, it proceeded to add: "Now, when our country is independent and proceeding well with its Five Years plans for development, there is no need for a large army. The youth needs to be provided jobs so as to keep them busy and productive. Nehruji has a Planning Commission and he has laid strong foundations for industrial growth. Jobs will emerge, and soon people will appreciate the fruits of planned development. Several IITs, numerous, new universities and research institutes and, a few IIMs have also been opened to train the youth and turn them employable."

Masterji wasn't very happy seeing his great hero attempting to satisfy and/or mollify him. Frustration took over, and he took out few grains of imported American wheat and, opening his palm towards the blackboard, retorted:

> *"Look, this is what we get to eat today; this hard and unpalatable wheat is imported under the PL-480 program. Our local wheat's yield is very small and food stocks of farmers normally finish by October/November each year. And then, they have to depend upon ration shops where only this imported wheat is available. If you were here as our leader, I am sure we would have been spared this humiliation."*

The great hero's soul measured the situation; it understood the gravity of the matter. Since answer must reach the agitated fan, in a subdued but hugely convincing tone it added:

> *"Masterji, you are a well-read person; you know the situation that the world faces today. No other country, except America, has surplus food—and no one else would give it almost free of cost. The countries with which I had contact are struggling with their own post-war shortages; neither Germany nor Japan could have spared food for India. And Russia, due to its collective farming mania, is in a severe production crisis. So, were I the Prime Minister of India, then America wouldn't have spared even a kilo of wheat for us. And for most of the Indians, it would have been a case of perpetual half-empty bellies. Americans didn't like me and my INA for fighting along with their arch enemy—the Japanese. It is, indeed, good that I am not there. Agreed, the quality of American wheat isn't to our liking, but at least the basic hunger of the Indian masses is being satisfied."*

And the great soul continued to add:

> *"Masterji, you must be remembering the Great Bengal Famine, when people on Calcutta streets and side-walks died like flies—hungry, diseased and neglected. No revolutionary could help to avert the situation. And if I were the first PM of India, wouldn't the situation have been worse than what it is today? For sure, I wouldn't have done as good a job as my friend Nehru has done. He is doing his best; importing what is available and on the other hand, encouraging farmers to produce more."*

Without a break, he added:

> *"Nehru's government is erecting several large dams and building new canals. Soon, there will be more irrigation that is bound to raise India's own local food grains output. Things will improve, I am sure," elaborated the great soul, adding, "The century's long neglect and exploitation by the imperialistic British regime had turned our people dry of initiative and entrepreneurship. It will take a while to correct the situation."*

Masterji got the point. He reluctantly seemed to agree with what his hero said. But he still had several queries and disappointments. He thought that he must clear as many as possible of his misgivings.

"See Netaji, what a mess Nehruji has created in case of the Jammu and Kashmir issue. Firstly, he delayed sending troops to repel the invaders. And then, he halted the operation midway. And as if it wasn't bad enough, he took the case to UNO. That institution is dominated by Western powers which never wanted India to be free—and now they don't want us to progress. Britain loves Pakistan as it is the baby of the West. We are going to have a permanent problem. What do you think of it? Wouldn't you have handled the situation better?" Masterji demanded to know.

Masterji's hero was quick to respond because military matters interested him the most. And he eagerly answered:

"Yes, in such matters, I could have done much better. First of all, I would have sent the military to stop the invaders without any delay. And my army wouldn't have stopped before recovering the whole territory. There would have been no question of letting the West-dominated UNO do anything in this matter. And there was no question of inserting article 370 in our Constitution to give special status to Jammu and Kashmir. I would have integrated the state fully into the Indian Union, despite protests if any."

Now, Masterji looked a lot better satisfied. He moved his mulberry twig in a manner that indicated his growing satisfaction, as a masterly interrogator.

"This is why we miss you a great deal. Our expectations of several decades have been lost for your inappropriate decision of electing not to come and take control of our newly liberated nation. Gandhiji, the Father of the Nation ditched us too. In a way, we are now in an orphan state," lamented Masterji, adding, "There is nobody around to exert needed moral control on our newly liberated politicians. They are falling prey to corruption and inefficiency. Their ego and greed is growing exponentially every day. How will we make them stick to some moral moorings? How will we make them work for the people?"

The great hero's soul attempted to satisfy its fan but wasn't very successful. The logic of a non-being attempting to deal with its dis-satisfied fan wasn't cutting much ice with a devotee who faced challenging situations on daily basis. And his situation often turned precarious because, being a Masterji, many people looked for his advice and guidance.

In the meantime, some other thoughts bubbled in Masterji's mind and without loss of any momentum he asked: "Tell me honestly; did Nehruji stop you from coming to India? I hear so many people saying that or, at least, implying so. Even some members of your large family have implied so. What is the truth? Tell me clearly."

It was a difficult question for our great hero. It seemed to carry a load of political implications. Masterji was indeed good at throwing probing queries—and the great soul being under obligation to answer all queries of its fan couldn't avoid replying howsoever difficult the queries.

Gathering conviction, it said:

> *"Look Masterji, in my actions, I have never been a weakling. Nobody could push me around. Britishers couldn't do a damn thing to me. And the Japanese, too, had a tough time in dealing with me. I held my head high and did what I wanted. So how could Nehru have stopped me from coming to India? I don't understand how such mean thoughts ingress minds of some people? It is my country; I have fought for it. And Nehru was never my enemy. He was my colleague in Congress for long years that I spent working for it. We were both leftists. We worked together on various issues. Yes, sometimes we had differences; in political maneuverings, things are never fully straight. But that is acceptable. He never came in my way. After I took that non-functional flight on August 18, 1945, I straightaway went to the Brahmaloka. Nehru was never to blame for it," said the great soul.*

"In fact, as all of you know, he very ably defended my soldiers of INA when they were tried at the historic Red Fort. I am indeed grateful for the skillful defense of my soldiers that he undertook. He wasn't practicing law for long years yet, for this great event, he stood up in a splendid manner. Please Masterji, don't blame him for my own failures," added the soul.

Masterji was taken aback by the candid expressions of his hero. His opinion was different. Possibly, it was biased or had turned illogical under the load of emotions. But one thing was crystal clear to Masterji—his hero had failed on some fronts. In addition to the military failure at the Indo-Burma border—where his laboriously assembled INA disintegrated in face of allied resistance—as a great warrior, he failed to surrender along with his combatants. It was a sour point in Masterji's understanding of his great hero's performance. He wanted to clarify the issue. Hence, he demanded:

> *"I know your INA lost to the superior resources of allied forces at the battles of Imphal and Kohima, but as a warrior general, why didn't you surrender along with your soldiers? It would have kept their moral high on one hand, and your dignity intact as a commander, on the other."*

It was a difficult question for the great hero to tackle. Nobody had ever dared to ask such an inconvenient question to him. He suspected that his great fan was testing him and, with the objective of not failing in his fan's test, he responded:

> *"Masterji, it is good that you raised this question. It has been stressing me for long. I haven't been at peace with myself about it. Yes, I should have surrendered along with my INA soldiers and their brave commanders. Not doing so wasn't an easy decision to arrive at. A mistake was made and I have often regretted the same. And had I done that, then there was no need for me to take a flight to Manchuria—which instead landed me in the Brahamaloka. My own mistake caused so much pain to my fans and family members," the great soul admitted painfully.*

Masterji appreciated the honesty of his hero and looked ready to ignore some lapses on his part. But many things still lingered in his mind. Several of his colleagues often asserted that Netaji was a fascist; he worked with them in Europe as well as in East Asia—and took their help too. Masterji thought that it was the right time to get some clarifications on the issue right from horse's mouth. He raised his voice and synchronously the stick in his right hand, too, went up as he demanded:

> *"I thought you were a righteous man. I mean, a man of principles.*

Why did you run to fascists for help, for freeing India from grip of imperialist Britain? You were aware of nationalists and revolutionaries in Ireland, Turkey, Cuba and China and that of several other countries where locals organized themselves without drawing upon outside help in freeing themselves from oppressive rulers. Why didn't you organize locally? Why didn't you convert your **'Forward Bloc'** *into a covert fighting force? Were we short of young men to join a fighting start-up—or the local businesses were reluctant to fund such a liberation movement?"*

He continued to ask: "Isn't a man known by the company he keeps? Won't you be known by your company of fascists and dictators?"

Masterji's questions were indeed loaded… some of which weren't easy to respond to. The great hero's soul felt that it had been away from the Brahamaloka for several Earth hours. Realizing complexity of the situation, the divine soul said:

'I have been out of my divine location for several Earth hours. You seem tired as well; we shall meet tomorrow here at the same time. In the meantime, I shall ponder over your deep queries."

And with this, the conversation fell silent.

Masterji retreated to his small office, and the students who were hiding under the benches too felt a moment of relief.

Masterji hardly slept in the night; the questions that he had raised continued to rotate in his mind. His illiterate wife suspected that something was amiss with the Panditji. For the past several days, he hadn't eaten well, and he had ignored the prayer time too. She hesitantly probed the situation by stating:

"What is troubling you, Masterji? Are students not listening to you? Or has the inspector who came to visit the school played some dirty game with you? Tell me, I am feeling uneasy..."

Masterji, too, wanted to talk. He wanted some load off his head.

Talking to the soul of his hero wasn't easy. It was indeed a taxing effort. And now that Masterni had raised the question, it became a lot easier to share what had happened to him.

Slowly and a little cautiously, he said:

"Masterni, today my hero's soul came to visit me. We have been talking about a few things, but rest assured, nothing was serious."

She knew who Masterji's hero was. Hence, without delay she demanded:

"You mean Netaji? The whole world knows that he died in a plane crash, some 10 years ago. How can he come to talk to you?" she demanded.

"Yes, it's him! With my great hero, I have been discussing some urgent issues!" Masterji elaborated.

"Don't lie!"She said, a little irritated. "Don't cheat me, Masterji. Tell me the truth," she added, slightly raising her voice.

It was unusual. Masterni had never raised her voice in the past. And Masterji, who was always the boss—at the school as well as at home—thought that it was better to tell her the truth.

"Look Masterni, I am telling the truth. Netaji's soul comes to talk to me and clarify why he didn't come to India and become our Prime Minister. It has now been a few days that we have been talking—and we will talk for some more days. The conversation is long and arduous. I am telling the truth. He is my hero; he can't refuse answering me," Masterji elaborated.

"He is my icon too; I am coming with you tomorrow morning to meet him," announced Masterni.

"No, you can't. He has agreed only to talk to me in complete privacy and solitude. He comes in soul form; one can't see him. Only I can talk to him," retorted Masterji.

"Can't you call your hero here? When you talk to him, I will just listen. And I will hide under my cot," she suggested.

Masterji was in a fix. He can't violate the condition which he had agreed with his great hero's soul. And Masterni seemed to be getting adamant. He couldn't afford annoying her too. A quick thought emerged and he suggested:

"OK, if you are adamant, then I would suggest a way out. You go to school half an hour early and hide under my desk in the classroom. No one should see you. And there, stay completely silent. I will keep the session short so that it's not too inconvenient for you. And you have to be in complete disguise of a cleaning woman. As our conversation ends, you wait for a few minutes and then quietly come back home."

Masterni agreed with the plan. Early next morning, she dressed as a cleaning woman and, donning a veil and a broom, reached the school premises when no one was there yet. She made herself comfortable under Masterji's large table. As usual, the classroom wasn't locked. The whole school, in fact, seemed under guard of a stray dog that had made itself comfortable under Masterji's desk.

Masterni cleared the place a little and spread a torn jute mattress under the table—and then slipped on to it. The table was pulled a little more near to the wall so that no one could glance under it.

At the appointed time, Masterji walked in, waving his mulberry stick in small circles and incomprehensively talking to himself. And the boys who regularly eavesdropped at the conversation, too, were under the benches well in time. They didn't see the cleaning woman under Masterji's table. Her camouflage was complete.

After entering the classroom, Masterji glanced to confirm that Masterni was well-hidden under his table. He didn't sit on his chair but straightway went to the blackboard, wrote Netaji on the blackboard a few times and raising his stick saying:

"I am ready to hear your explanation, my hero. I have come well in time. I don't like delaying anything. Tell me the truth about the matter that I raised last with you yesterday," he demanded, looking at the blackboard.

The divine response was quick:

"Masterji, let me first explain about me being a man of principles. My principle is simple—my objective of pushing the British out of India was sacrosanct. It was non-negotiable. And I wanted to employ

the force of weapons for achieving the objective. Unlike Mahatma Gandhi, I never suffered the confusion of ways and means. I never believed in the sanctity of means. I believed in sanctity of my objectivity. I was never a Gandhian in true sense of the term. I had joined Congress because it was the only effective force at that time which had some chance of forcing the Raj authorities to have a rethink."

"With regard to ways and means, I am more near to ***Lord Krishna***[7], who believed that while fighting an invincible enemy, some non-dharma means could be employed. When the invincible guru Drona had to be done away, he made Yodhisthira utter a lie. For it, the latter suffered loss of conscience but the battle of Kurukchetra was given a winning turn," added the great hero's soul.

"In 1940s, I had no choice. Not many powers in the world were in a position to raise a voice against the imperialistic Britain. Its political and military clout was large, and resources even larger. Only axis powers namely Italy, Germany and Japan didn't agree with Britain—and Russia, at least initially, looked neutral. With lot of efforts, presentations and cajoling on my part, Germans showed some interest to help Indians. But they soon made a mistake of attacking Russia, and got weakened in the process. And Britain, on the other hand, got emboldened when USA decided to side with the anti-fascist Europeans. The Japanese folly of attacking USA at the Pearl Harbor pulled the latter into the Great War."

The great hero's soul was in a dialogue mood, and it further added:

"I was aware that revolutions in Turkey, Ireland, Cuba and China were primarily based upon indigenous resources. But I had no skills of that type; I wasn't a trained military man and with wide eyes and sharp ears of Raj authorities, it looked difficult to provoke and process an indigenous armed revolution."

Masterji was uncomfortable with the explanation and he butted in to say:

"I have always respected your nationalistic commitments and opinions but, in this case, I have no option except disagreeing with you."

"With your skills of dialogue, there couldn't have been any shortage of young men to join your cause. And I am sure, a lot of traders and businessmen in India would have been ready to finance your mission. And there wasn't any dearth of weaponry. It could be imported, or police stations could have been looted. There was sympathy for your cause amongst the majority of Indian army personnel. Many of them could have sided with you. Tell me, why didn't you choose to raise a guerilla force right here in the country? It didn't need much skill," questioned Masterji.

The great soul sensed being trapped by its investigative fan. It quickly surmised that it was always better to be truthful—and oriented to say:

"Yes Masterji, the option of going with a covert war looked difficult to me. I thought that I could do a good job with help of my communist and fascist friends. But in hindsight, it looks like it wasn't a very sound route. In this case, there was a very heavy dependence on others while a covert war could have been fully under my control."

Masterji was greatly pleased with a truthful answer from his hero. It furthered his already deep respect for him. Before Masterji could ask any new question, the great soul elected to further elaborate:

"Your apprehensions about my company of fascists, too, are genuine. People do surmise that the company of fascists might have affected me. Rightly or wrongly, the association did have some impact on my thought process. But now that I am in the Brahamaloka, it doesn't really matter. Our great Lord and his management over here do not discriminate based on such grounds."

Masterji wasn't fully satisfied with the divine reply, but he didn't want to further probe the delicate issue. Hence, changing the discussion, he asked:

"What about your '**Forward Bloc**' *followers?" They were assembled by you with great conviction?"*

"Why they couldn't be employed for a covert struggle?" Masterji demanded to know.

It was again a difficult probe by a committed fan. But the great hero's soul couldn't afford to skip the query; it was under a commitment that had to be honored at all costs.

"Masterji, telling you the truth, the Forward Blocists were political elements. They could raise loud slogans. They weren't fighters. And being urbanites, they couldn't fit into a jungle life that becomes an essential part of a covert operation. I didn't take risk with them. Most of them were political opportunists; they wanted to operate on my energies. They didn't have any self-propulsion. Fascists, at least, were committed to their anti-British orientation. In my view, even a committed evil is better than uncommitted and unreliable saint," elaborated the great hero.

Masterni twisted and turned under the table, but she didn't mind the discomfort because the conversation between Masterji and the divine soul of his hero was indeed interesting. She had never listened to a divine soul. She wasn't brought up in an environment of superstition. Although illiterate, her thoughts were logical and almost scientific. Listening to a conversation between Masterji and his hero's soul interested her a great deal.

While Masterji seemed content with what his hero said, he hurried up to ensure that the guest soul didn't leave in a hurry. Some of his queries still agitated in his head. He wanted to do full justice with the great opportunity to know the truth. Hence, he hurried up to ask:

> *"Did you have a tendency to predict outcomes without adequate analysis? You said in early 1940s that the European fascists were poised to win the WW II. What was the use of making such predictions? The control of war in Europe wasn't in your hands, and the powers involved in the conflict hadn't sure confided in you about their plans and the resources at their command. Did you want to just impress your collaborators? From East Asia, too, in radio talks you often gave an impression that the Axis forces were about to liberate India. You hadn't factored for the power of Americans. Were you not a propagandist?" Masterji demanded to know.*

It was a loaded question again. Even otherwise, in a situation of no win or say defeat, it is always difficult to answer causes of failures. Masterji was a hard examiner of facts; he didn't want to be lenient with his hero. Who was at the other side didn't matter to him. Seeing the discomfort of his hero's soul, the great examiner said: "You can skip the question if it is too difficult, or too personal."

"Now that I am not in a physical form, there is no difficulty in answering any type of question. No one can blame me now," asserted the great hero's soul. "Let me admit that I made predictions which didn't come true. My objective of making the same was genuinely nationalistic—i.e. to turn opinion against allied powers in general, and the British in particular. It was part of my strategy to keep my benefactors in good humour," elaborated the soul.

"Yes, I had a tendency to go for propaganda. I made great radio speeches from Europe as well as from the East Asia. It was plausibly the Germans' approach that influenced me. Also, at that time, it seemed to me that my propaganda did hurt the British leaders and the Raj apparatus in India. At that time, it gave me immense pleasure but now, with the hindsight, I think that observance of restraint would have been a better choice," explained the great soul.

"I am happy to see that you are being self-critical," interjected Masterji.

Masterni was getting increasingly uncomfortable under the table. And Masterji, too, was feeling hungry as in her excitement to hear her husband's conversation with his great hero, she hadn't made any breakfast this morning. She must get back home and cook for Masterji. It was already lunch time. Realizing the situation, the great fan of our hero suggested: "We have been talking for a few hours. I am also feeling hungry. And someone might also be missing you in the Brahamaloka. So, we meet tomorrow at the same time. That will be our last session. And I may not bother you afterwards with my troublesome queries."

"It is OK with me. I don't get the opportunity to talk to my devoted fans every day. And your intense queries have stimulated some new thought processes in my mind. I wish you had talked to me before August 18, 1945 event that brought me to Brahamaloka," the great hero's soul admitted frankly.

Masterni was happy on two counts. Firstly, her ordeal of hiding under a table was over. Secondly, for the first time in her life she heard a divine voice talk to her husband. And finally, she now appreciated her husband's capacity for critical examination, a lot better. For her, it was now a matter of pride that her husband, a mere Masterji, could talk to divine voices.

She quietly moved out of the classroom and Masterji went to his office for attending to normal activities of the primary school. He, too, looked satisfied on the turn of events. And the students who were hiding under benches on back of the classroom scrambled out and moved quietly to their class as well. They were scared that if Masterji comes to know of their misadventure, they sure would be terminated from the school. There was no other school within 10-km radius. Since the matter was interesting, they took the risk.

Udai, the senior-most of them, had taken notes of the whole conversation. While carefully hiding the notebook in his school bag, he said to himself:

> *"This notebook is very valuable. I can't take the risk of someone pinching it out of my bag. Tomorrow, I will bring a new notebook and put this one safely away in my old books' trunk. No one will notice it there."*

Masterni, on way back home, thought of Brahamaloka. She argued with herself: "If I reach Brahamaloka, I can talk to Masterji whenever I want. And can also trace my mother in some corners of the divine space. Won't it be good? And I shall need to do no house work there; no fetching water from the well and no grinding and cooking! It would be a beautiful life. And there won't be any mother-in-law to scold me. I will be a free bird doing only what interests me. But I must ask Masterji when he comes home for lunch as to how to reach the divine space of Brahamaloka."

Soon, she reached home. Her mother-in-law was at the door; the old lady looked furious. She, too, had gone without meals today. It had never happened earlier. And as Masterni entered the house, a sharp confrontation welcomed her:

"Where were you whole the forenoon? I am hungry. Even buffaloes are without water and fodder," she grumbled.

"I went on a divine mission. I am tired of working here the whole day and listening to your acidic barbs. I went to find a way of going to Brahamaloka where things are comfortable and one is under divine grace whole the time," replied Masterni while getting busy with her pending house work.

The old lady was startled by her daughter-in-law's talk of going to Brahamaloka.

"Who will look after the household, the buffaloes and my son? I am old and Masterji doesn't know anything about house work, or about taking care of the animals. His life revolves around his school. Who has put this devilish idea in your mind?" the old lady demanded to know.

"I don't know; I have had enough of this house work. These buffaloes, I didn't bring as dowry. And in any case, I am a barren woman. I haven't given you grandchildren. After I am gone, Masterji can marry again and you can have an army of brats," Masterni spoke out of accumulated disgust.

The old lady was beaten at her own argument. Masterni was in high spirits. Now, Brahamaloka was her destination. Only she was looking for a short and sweet way of reaching there. She hoped Masterji will guide her.

While her thoughts ran wild, she busied herself physically with preparation of simple lunch of dal and roti. There was plenty of milk and homemade butter to smoothen the affair. Besides, she was getting disinterested in chores of daily life.

It was half-past two in the afternoon when a famished Masterji walked in. Masterni was ready with two *thalis*, one for the old mother-in-law and another for Masterji. There was no dining table in the house; Masterji sat on an **'asana'** placed on the cow-dung plastered kitchen floor. And the old lady retreated to the interior of the house; she wanted to eat alone and not disturb her son.

While serving the food to her husband, Masterni said:

"I was greatly impressed by your hero; he gave all the answers. He looks comfortable in the Brahamaloka. I am keen to go there."

Masterji ignored the query; he wanted to finish with the lunch and then have a small nap. Masterni raised the issue again—this time by complaining about her mother-in-law's taunts.

"Your mother always insults me. She says I am a barren land; no seed sprouts in me. I don't know how far it's my fault. And I want to free you; you can marry again. I will go to Brahamaloka and be with my loving mother. Just tell me how to go there," Masterni desired to know.

Without reacting, he had his lunch. Masterji was aware of the conflict between the two women of the house. On way to the siesta, he attempted to assuage Masterni's hurt, as he said: "We will discuss the issue in the evening. I am not walking back to the school this afternoon. I have sent everybody home. It's a half-day holiday at the school. Wake me up at 4:30 pm with tea."

She agreed with Masterji and, after a quick lunch, busied herself with the care of animals. Buffaloes had to be fed and bathed so that they were ready to give milk in the evening. The cattle-shed had to be cleaned and dung/rubbish carted away to the compost pit. It was a lot of hard work. Although she was losing interest in this kind of work, she hurried through it as there wasn't an alternative.

Exactly at 4:30, she carried a wooden tray with tea pot and a cup to Masterji.

Masterji could snatch no rest from the siesta on account of his wife's perplexing question. He wasn't able to restrain his mother from throwing taunts at his wife who suffered a great deal. He was aware of her torments and frustrations.

Before his wife could refresh her query, Masterji said: "I don't know the way to Brahamaoka except that one has to die for any success in that direction. You are too young for a journey to the divine space. But if you insist, I would ask my great hero during my planned conversation with him tomorrow. May be there is a simpler way," he added with the thought of diverting his disturbed wife's inquisitiveness.

"Please do ask him. Since Netaji is your hero, I don't want to ask him directly," she concurred.

Masterji's students, except Udai, had just a light interest in his talk with the great hero's soul but curiosity kept them into the game. Next morning, the group of youngsters, as usual, reached the school well in time. Udai with his new notebook was the first to go under the benches; he was ready to take notes of the next divine conversation. Today, possibly, was the final divine dialogue.

Masterji walked in with a swagger, waving his mulberry stick aimlessly. As he raised it standing against the blackboard, the Brahamaloka connection came alive.

He hadn't even written anything on the blackboard. His hero's soul was just waiting for its fan's presence. How the great soul and Masterji wished each other wasn't audible but soon, the latter was heard saying: "Netaji, I have several queries still left with me but, for paucity of time, I will raise only the prime ones i.e. for which my friends and colleagues are most interested to get explanations."

"What intrigues me and my friends most is that your large family is greatly divided about the mystery/controversy of your death /or disappearance on August 18, 1945. Why is it so? Why can't they agree about facts? Or why don't you ask them not to complicate the situation? Some, including your daughter Anita, agree that you died in the plane crash. Others, who are a majority, don't agree and assert that you faked your death with assistance, or in connivance with the Japanese authorities. Now, even when you yourself confirm that you are in Brahamaloka, some of them insist that you never died and that for long years you were in disguise or in a self-imposed exile somewhere in Russia or Central Asia. Others propagate that you lived in India as a 'Gumnami Baba' in a small town of Northern India. Why is there such confusion?" Masterji demanded a final clarity.

This personal and long query made the great soul fumble a little. And after recollecting itself, went ahead to explain:

"What my daughter Anita said is the real fact. She had no interest in twisting the same. Several members of the large Bose family had varied political interests, distributed over almost all the political parties of democratic India. Congress, Communists, and the Forward Bloc have been their political playgrounds and in future new ones, namely Trinamool Congress and BJP, would attract their political associations. Opportunism rather than principles or ideology would be the guiding line. And accordingly, their statements are bound to vary from time to time. Have I made the situation clear, Masterji?" demanded the great soul.

Masterji was satisfied and he said: "I am happy with the clarity that you have imparted to my thinking. I have taken your valuable time."

"Now that I am in the divine space, I have no shortage of time. And let me tell you...I value a lot the feelings and aspirations of my fans," summarized the great soul.

"But before I let you go, I have one more query. May be you can help!" said Masterji as if he were in a hurry. "My wife wants to know whether there is a simpler way to reach the divine space of Brahamaloka? She is keen to go there and be with her mother," Masterji added.

"Masterji, I don't know of any simpler route to this place. One isn't allowed to come here in his or her physical form. It has to be discarded as a primary requirement," clarified the great hero's soul.

And the two rolled up their conversation.

Udai, too, stopped scribbling in the new notebook.

Masterji was first to leave the classroom. He was in a motivated form as the conversation with the divine had invigorated him.

The students, too, were out from under the benches. The rest of the day at the school was uneventful.

On return journey, the students had a fill from the guava orchards and returned home happily. And thereafter, Udai's two notebooks remained in safe custody for several decades.

Jai Hind

Abbreviations Employed

BJP	Bhartiya Janta Party—a right wing political party of India
BSP	Bahujan Samaj Party—serving primarily political interests of dalits in India
FB	Forward Bloc—a leftist political outfit started by Subhash Bose after leaving Congress
IB	Intelligence Bereau—an investigation and information gathering agency
ICS	Indian Civil Service
INA	The Indian National Army or the Azad Hind Fauz of Subhash Bose
INC	The Indian National Congress
NDA	National Democratic Alliance—a grouping of political parties with the BJP being in the lead
POLC	A management term employed to describe the planning and management process.
RSS	Rastriya Savamsevak Sangh—a right wing Hindutva promoting organization
RTI	Right to information Act
SWOT	A management analysis tool that analises strengths, weaknesses, opportunities and threats to any project and/ or operation

TMC	Trinamool Congress—a political party
UPA	United Progressive Alliance—a center and left oriented alliance of political parties with the Congress in the lead
WW I	World War One—fought in middle and late 1910s
WW II	The second world war—fought between the Axis forces and Allied powers between 1939 and 1945.

Jai Hind

THE TIMELINES OF BOSE'S LIFE

Date	**Year**	**Event**
January 23	1897	Was born to Parbhavati and Jankinath Bose as 6th child in a large group of 11 children
	1916	Was expelled from Presidency College, Calcatta for nationalistic activities
	1919	Earned in BA Philosophy from Scottish Church College, Calcutta
	1919	Joined Fitzwilliam College at Cambridge
May	1921	Returned to India after passing ICS and soon resigned from the service
July	2921	Met Gandhiji and was influenced a great deal
	1923	Joined the Indian National Congress and became commandant of Congress volunteers
	1924	Appointed as Chief Executive Officer of Calcutta Corporation when C R Das was its mayor
September	1930	Became Mayor of Calcutta.
June	1935	Met Benito Mussolini of Italy.
	1938	Elected as INC President
April	1939	Resigned from as President of INC
May	1939	Founded Forward Bloc

July	1940	Was arrested
January	1941	Escaped to Europe from house-arrest
April	1942	British banned the Forward Bloc
	1942	Bose married Emillie Schenki. Reported to have married secretly right in 1937.
November	1942	A daughter named Anita was born
May	1943	Submarine journey to East Asia; reached Tokyo in May 43.
	1943	Took over charge of INA
October	1943	Proclaimed establishment of Provisional Government of India
March	1944	Along with Japanese his INA advanced to Rangoon and entered soon India
August 18	1945	Died in plane crash at Taipei
March	1946	Emillie informed Sarat Chandra Bose thru a letter that she had married Subhash

Jai Hind

NOTES AND CLARIFICATIONS

(i) The Indian media, national as well as regional, on 24th January 2016 morning seemed furiously competing with each other in regards to report on what was seen in the files, or heard about them. The Times of India covered one full page, detailing various tidbits available from the declassified files. In brief, the media seemed disappointed with the outcome as well as with efforts of the BJP government to appropriate the iconic hero's legacy.

(ii) Netaji's grand-nephew named Surya Kumar Bose gave an interview to the Times of India which was reports in its 27th January, 2016, edition. He answered a dozen question and what emerged out of it included: (a) that the Modi government was the only one that had courage to declassify the files, (b) his accumulated anger against Congress came out flowing freely, and (c) he seemed to accuse the Congress that it was always bent upon proving that Bose died in the plane crash of August 1945, while for him it wasn't a fact. He covered up the Modi government's strategically timing the release of files in view of upcoming West Bengal elections. He said that the Khoshla Commission set up in 1970 was a farce. That the Bose family members who entered Parliament were sharply critical of Congress, primarily for not supporting the non-fact that Bose hadn't died in the said air crash. The intension of the Bose family to keep the controversy alive became further clarifies—they now wanted all the files in related countries to be opened too. And the rumor that he was to join BJP before the coming West Bengal election too got highlighted.

(iii) A PTI news report reproduced in the 14th February edition of *"The Hindu."*

(iv) The Indian Express date-lined 25th January, 2016, published a detailed interview of a pro-disappearance myth advocate of the Bose family. He made baseless insinuation on the Congress or Gandhi-Nehru family.

(v) The Asian Age in its 25th January, 2016 issue, amongst others, commented, "....but it's an irony that despite the files now being public no clear evidence has emerged on whether the iconic hero who waged war to free his country survived or died in the 1945 air crash near Taipei. Only one 1945 Cabinet note states his death took place, but without any new evidence."

(vi) Tehelka' s special New Year (2016) issue carried an article titled "The Nehru-Netaji Splitsville" by Sarija Naskar which highlighted Bose family's misgivings and accusations about Nehru having grabbed what rightfully was that of Netaji's.

(vii) A report in the Times of India dated 16 March, 2016 dealt in detail about Gumnami Baba, his secret life and resemblance with Bose.

(vii) A report in the Times of India dated 16 March, 2016 detailed some RSS leaders lamentations that they didn't act in time to help Bose.

Jai Hind

References

1. Marshal J Getz (2002) "Subhash Chandra Bose: A Biography" published by McFarland & Company, Inc, North Carolina 28640.
2. Subhash Chandra Bose, an Indian Pilgrim: An Unfinished Autobiography and Collection of Letters, 1897-1921 (Calcutta, 1965), pp1-3.
3. J B Kripalani, "My Times: An Autobiography" published by Rupa&Co, Ansari Road, Daryaganj, New Delhi 110002, pp361
4. Barbara D. Metcalf and Thomas R. Metcalf (2004), "A Concise History of India 2nd edition" Cambridge University Press—ISBN 978 0521 6822 51.
5. Suyin Han and Jonathan Cape (1972), "Dedication," The Morning Deluge, Mao Tsetung and the Chinese Revolution, 1893-1953, London: 30 Bedford Square, Chapter2, p-44.
6. Poonam Surie (2015), "China: Confucius in the Shadows." KW Publishers Pvt. Ltd. 4676, Daryaganj, New Delhi 110002
7. U V Singh (2008), "Management Wisdom of Lord Krishna," published by New Century Publications, Ansari Road, New Delhi 110002.

Jai Hind